What People Are Saying About Melvin Pillay

"Melvin, I love your enthusiasm. What a privilege it is for you to be here with us, where you also honored God so wonderfully well and so excitingly."

—Zig Ziglar

"Melvin Pillay is a gifted life coach who knows how to unlock the best out of any individual with love and care."

—Ambassador Samuel Fidelis

"Understanding success is one of the major challenges of today's world. Melvin Pillay shares how to gain true success not only at work but also at home. This teaching results from Melvin's practical living, which came from more than twenty-five years of research on this topic."

—Tamrat Layne, Former Prime Minister of Ethiopia

"Melvin Pillay is a rare find. For all who read these words, I hope that you have at least one chance to encounter Melvin sometime in your life."

—Perry Marshall

Melvin's work as a speaker and mentor has already transformed hundreds, if not thousands, of lives. As more embrace the wisdom gleaned in The Smart Work Matrix, the potential for millions, if not billions, to experience life transformation is there to be unlocked.

—Lord Wei of Shoreditch, Member of the House of Lords of the United Kingdom

THE
SMART
WORK
MATRIX

UNLOCKING THE CODE TO BETTER MENTAL HEALTH, WELL-BEING AND PRODUCTIVITY

MELVIN PILLAY

Published by

www.ssalipublishing.africa   Proudly Amplifying the Voices of African Authors

In collaboration with

UNISA | university of south africa PRESS

Printed in the United States of America

ISBN 978-0-473-74249-2

TABLE OF CONTENTS

First, I was dying to finish high school and start college. And then I was dying to finish college and start working.

And then I was dying to marry and have children.

And then I was dying for my children to grow old enough for school so I could return to work.

And then I was dying to retire.

And now, I am dying... and suddenly, I realize I forgot to live.

- Anonymous

To all the hard workers of the past who were taught to reward hard work with more work—welcome to The Smart Work Matrix.

FOREWORD

In a world that often glorifies busyness and equates success with unrelenting effort, many of us find ourselves caught in an endless cycle of overwork. We live in an age where "hustle culture" permeates our daily lives, pushing us to work harder, longer, and faster. Yet, as the familiar saying goes, "Busy is not the same as productive."

This book invites you to embark on a transformative journey away from this all-too-common narrative. It introduces the concept of "The Smart Work Matrix," a revolutionary approach to work that champions balance, fulfillment, and, ultimately, a more meaningful life. This isn't just about working less; it's about working smarter— finding a pathway that doesn't require sacrificing your well-being or happiness.

In economics, we ask what it is you are maximizing. Economics does not care what the answer is because it lacks ethics and a soul. This book will ensure that you ask the right questions, like Socrates and Jesus. What is a good life? What is my purpose? How do I find meaning?

The journey towards a more liberated work-life balance is not just a personal one; it is a collective movement. Each of us has the power to redefine our relationship with work and, in doing so, inspire others to do the same. By adopting the strategies of "The Smart Work Matrix." The decision is yours, and it has the power to reshape not only your life but also the lives of those around you.

Welcome to a new beginning.

Dr. Dave Brat,

Former U.S. congressman, seminarian, professor, economist, and media personality. He served as the U.S. representative for Virginia's 7th congressional district, the Dean of the Liberty University School of Business, and now, SVP for Business Relations.

PREFACE

We were born to play.

When we were small, we were encouraged to play. People bought us toys and took us places to have fun, and we loved it.

Playing is innate, and it is no wonder—the benefits of play are numerous. Play improves cognitive, physical, social, and emotional well-being. In other words, playing makes one smarter, healthier, happier, more connected, and more accomplished.

One day, play was taken away from us with the words: Stop playing and act your age. You are not a child anymore. Get a job, work hard, and make something of your life.

Suddenly, life went from play to work, and our safe world changed from games to battles, from a playground to a war zone. Work became a fight.

Then, one day, you visited Grandma at the old people's home, and she was busy playing games and having fun because the experts said that playing had numerous benefits. They said:

Playing makes one smarter, healthier, happier, more connected, and more accomplished.

You scratch your head and wonder, *"Did I miss something?"* Children and older people are encouraged to play, but everybody else is told to *work* hard.

No wonder global health organizations say there is a significant increase in mental illness around the world. Stress levels are at an all-time high, and even with all our stuff and amazing technology, we are far less happy. Could the 1659 saying by J. Howell be right? Maybe it's even a prophecy: *All work and no play make Jack a dull boy.*

In Our Minds, in Our Mouths

The word *work* is common and frequently used in our daily conversations. For example, we say things like:

> This combination seems to *work.*

> I will check my calendar to see if that time will *work.*

> This partnership does not *work.*

> And of course, the big one—I am going to *work!*

From being young adults to becoming old people, our days are filled with work.

We go to work for ourselves.

We go to work for our children.

We go to work for others.

We go to work for survival.

It's time to play again, understand work, redefine success and fulfillment, and implement The Smart Work Matrix to enjoy better mental health, well-being, productivity, and a better way of life.

Melvin Pillay

INTRODUCTION

If hard work made one rich, the African woman
would be a billionaire.

- African Proverb

How we think about a certain thing as young children will be
how we view it throughout our lives and also how we live our
days on earth. This is called our state of mind, and it determines everything.

Retraining the Mind

From birth, every traumatic experience and harmful negative
thing leads to developing the brain's negative state of mind.
Conversely, positive and uplifting things lead to the brain's
positive state of mind. Therapists using cognitive behavioral
therapy (CBT) can help people change their state of mind by
getting them to practice positive emotions and positive emotional viewpoints so that an individual can break the pattern
of negative anticipation. This means our state of mind, which
is either negative or positive, can be taught to create new
anticipation.

Amazingly, our very thoughts often become our reality, thereby acting as self-fulfilling prophecies.

Our state of mind determines the outcome of our life.

We need to cultivate a positive rather than a negative state of mind. We will all encounter painful, life-altering moments. When you lose a loved one or something traumatic happens, it can put you in a state of grief or depressed emotions. But the longer you stay in that state, the harder it is for you to break out of it, and the more permanent that emotion becomes. A positive state of mind will help you overcome breakthroughs and break free faster from grief and emotional depression.

The State of Mind of Work

Another state-of-mind issue is toward work. Children view *work* as being hard and meaningless, a bad thing that takes Mom and Dad away.

> "We needed you, but you ignored us."

> "You even left us with strangers at daycares or with other relatives while you went to the place called 'work.'"

> "You could not give us your time; work took it all."

We witnessed our parents work hard, long hours, telling us, "I am doing it for you." And so, our state of mind about work was formed. We started to believe that hard work is productive and rest is unproductive. The longer this remained as our state of mind, the more permanent it became, and we created the anticipation of a life of hard work as a "good" thing.

In today's world, countless millions of individuals find themselves trapped in a suffocating existence, engulfed by a pervasive gloom that feels as heavy as death itself. Many are constrained by the relentless burden of hard work, shackled by the invisible but unyielding chains of misery and toil. These chains bind them physically and stifle their hopes and aspirations, leaving them yearning for liberation and a brighter future. It is evident that we have reached a critical juncture; it is time for us to break free from these oppressive circumstances and seek a more fulfilling and humane way of living and working that nurtures our spirits and fosters our potential.

CHAPTER ONE

CRACK THE SMART WORK MATRIX CODE

Overworking is more than just an issue; it frequently leads to a prevalent, accepted addiction known as workaholism. Many people find themselves trapped in its grip, believing that constant busyness equates to success. Laboring hard becomes a burden, weighing heavily on our spirits. Conversely, work absence can lead to stagnation and idleness, which we often label laziness. However, imagine a state of The Smart Work Matrix, a concept representing true liberation and victory.

The definition of work is to cultivate and manage, while hard work is often painful toil. For those who tend to think that hard work should always be reciprocated with even more work, it's time to rethink our approach. Let's explore a strategy that offers us freedom from this endless cycle of hard work. Discover how to embrace a life designed for ease and fulfillment, unshackled from the demands of relentless striving.

The Smart Work Matrix is a call to transform our perception of work, success, and fulfillment. See how it is changing the way people view success, empowering them to break free from the chains of overwork and reclaim their lives. Join the movement to redefine success and embrace a life of freedom and fulfillment.

Hard work or The Smart Work Matrix, that choice is yours alone.

CHAPTER TWO

SUCCESS VS VICTORY

One day, I found myself deep in thought, reflecting on the nature of human existence and why achieving a work-life balance is so challenging. It occurred to me that humankind is innately designed for triumph and fulfillment; however, we often become ensnared in the struggle for survival, which frequently transforms into an unending pursuit for success. This led me to question: Is there truly a distinction between success and victory?

As I contemplated this idea, the realization hit me with the force of a ton of bricks, illuminating the complexity of our journey. I recognized that our upbringing, cultural influences, and environmental factors profoundly shape our beliefs and aspirations. These forces often guide us toward the path of least or most resistance, influencing our choices and the direction of our lives.

I began to grasp that VICTORY is not merely an endpoint but a profound state characterized by a deep sense of accomplishment and fulfillment. It represents the crowning glory of human achievement, a moment when our efforts, sacrifices, and determination coalesce into something truly meaningful. Victory is a feeling that resonates from within, often rooted in personal values and aspirations.

In contrast, SUCCESS frequently manifests as a form of external validation, often tied to tangible accomplishments such as promotions, accolades, or milestones. While success can bring a rush of ego boost and temporary satisfaction, it tends to be fleeting and can easily slip away due to external factors beyond our control. This transient nature leaves us in a perpetual state of striving, constantly yearning for the next achievement to fill the void. This frequently leads to an unending quest, driven by desires that may never find complete fulfillment.

This nuanced distinction between victory and success ignited a deeper curiosity within me. I felt compelled to explore how our environments—cultural, social, and economic contexts— shape our definitions of success. I began to consider how these factors influence our capacity to recognize and attain true victory. This exploration not only reshaped my understanding of personal achievement but also deepened my appreciation for the intricate ways in which our surroundings mold our aspirations.

Performance vs Love

Inside each of us are two driving forces: one named Performance and the other named Love. Performance tends to follow the path of most resistance. It needs to be in control; therefore, when it does not get its way and loses control, it begins to worry about many things. Striving to maintain control and overextending its responsibilities often leads to worry, anxiety, fear, bondage, and paralysis of action. Love chooses to follow the path of least resistance. It is the better path; it is complete, content, fruitful, and victorious.

Yes, Performance and Love exist within us. They contend with each other, and the one that prevails is the one you nurture the most.

Human nature craves control, and the burden of hard work has transformed into a philosophy, a tradition, and now our reality. The desire for success enslaves us, and performance propels us. There is a profound difference between a person who is complete versus a person who is in control. Therefore, achieving work-life balance is impossible without confronting this burdensome philosophy.

The two diagrams on the following pages are designed to help you visualize and understand the contrasting journeys represented by The Path of Most Resistance and The Path of Least Resistance. By exploring these illustrations, you'll gain insights that will provide a clearer perspective on the choices before you.

The Path of Most Resistance

HARD WORK is based on success, which demands results that often make one egocentric and wanting to be in control. Performance is the driving force.

Inquisitive Reflections

1. What is the main theme of "The Path of Most Resistance"?
2. How can the pursuit of success lead to egocentric behavior?
3. Why is performance considered the driving force?

4. How can a desire for control affect relationships with others in a work environment?
5. How can one balance ambition and humility?

The Counterarguments

✓ How would you respond to someone who argues that hard work alone does not guarantee success and that external factors, such as socioeconomic background, also play a significant role?

✓ Have you considered the viewpoint that an emphasis on performance can lead to burnout and a lack of fulfillment, which ultimately undermines the idea of success?

✓ What would you say to critics who claim that defining success solely through results diminishes the value of personal growth and learning from failure?

The Path of Least Resistance

The Smart Work Matrix is based on victory, which gives fruit and makes one content and complete. Love is the driving force.

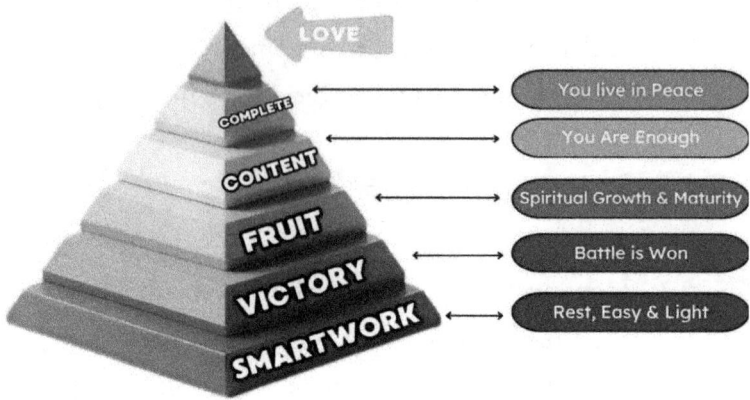

Inquisitive Reflections

1. What does "The Path of Least Resistance" suggest about decision-making and the approach to challenges in life?
2. How does the concept of "victory" within The Smart Work Matrix translate to personal fulfillment and happiness?
3. In what ways can love be seen as a driving force in achieving success and contentment?
4. What are some practical ways to embody the principles outlined in the text?
5. How might the ideas presented in the text influence one's perspective on failure and setbacks?

The Counterarguments

- ✓ How would you address those who argue that victory and success do not always lead to true contentment and fulfillment?
- ✓ What about the perspective that love can sometimes complicate or hinder the path to personal success?
- ✓ Can victory foster unhealthy competition rather than genuine satisfaction or completeness?

CHAPTER THREE

THE HARD WORKER

A thought of hard work becomes an emotion of hard work, which becomes words of hard work, ultimately becoming a life of hard work because of the philosophy spoken to us. We work so hard and cannot be free from the shackles of life.

Words are not meaningless; they bring either life or death. We are where and what we are because of the philosophy and blueprint of hard work. People work so hard because it has been spoken over them as children.

Hard work is the biggest lie, the biggest killer of dreams, and the biggest burden in this world. Most of us can relate to growing up in an environment that taught us the philosophy of hard work.

Seven things were spoken over us ever since we were children. The words may be spoken differently in your house, but the concepts are the same:

> #1 My child, work hard in school so that you can get good grades and go to college.

#2 My child, work hard in college so that you can get good grades and get a good job.

#3 My child, work hard at your job so that you will earn good money and get married.

#4 My child, marriage is tough, but you must work hard at your marriage.

#5 My child, have children of your own, but remember that children are hard work.

#6 My child, work hard to be a good parent so you can give your children the best.

#7 My child, do not talk to strangers and do not ask for money; work hard, be nice to everyone, and teach your children to do the same.

Like sheep going to the slaughter, we unwittingly follow these unwritten laws of life, ensnared by their vicious cycles and drudgery. And with pinpoint accuracy, they are fulfilled in our lives—we are saddled from generation to generation with the burden of hard work.

School became hard work, and college became hard work. Our job became hard work. Our marriage became hard work. Our children became hard work. We did not talk to strangers and missed all the great opportunities. We did not ask for money and missed all the additional sales and pay raises that were rightfully ours. We worked hard and became nice people, timid and plagued by the fear of rejection, fear of failure, and the fear of what others think of us.

Then, somewhere around the age of sixty-five to seventy, we are told that we are now too old and it's time to retire, give up on our dreams, and get ready to die. And not once did we ask the question *why!*

Why must school be hard work?

Why must college be hard work?

Why must my job be hard work?

Why must my marriage be hard work?

Why must my children be hard work?

Why must my life be hard work?

But now, everything has changed. There is a better way to live. We have The Smart Work Matrix.

CHAPTER FOUR

THE TEN STRATEGIES

There is a profound difference between work and hard work.

Hard work is warfare, and people have to fight for survival. Therefore, we call it the hustle or the grind and use idioms like "blood, sweat, and tears," "backs to the grindstone," and "burning the candle at both ends." It's what I call being a conqueror. But we can be more than conquerors. This funny illustration will elaborate on my point a bit more.

The Two Boxers

Two heavyweight boxers were fighting for the title of Heavyweight Champion of the World. Both were formidable fighters. They went after each other; round after round, they battled. Through the pain and the toil, the blood, the sweat, and the tears, they fought for their bread. Finally, the faster man struck the other on the jaw and knocked him out. The crowd cheered, and the bell rang. The referee announced the winner by a knockout. They placed the check in the hands of the winner; he was the conqueror. He went home and placed the check in his wife's hands; she was more than the conqueror.

Our greatest victories come from the battles we do not fight.

- The burden of hard work is given to those who must battle as conquerors.
- The privilege of Smart Work is given to those who are more than conquerors.

Hard Work is a philosophy of fighting for success. Smart work is a philosophy of living in victory. Let us adopt and embody the ten strategies of the Smart Work Matrix.

Strategy One - Create

Reframe your understanding of work; it transcends the notion of a physical location and becomes a continuous engagement of the mind. When you immerse yourself in deep thought and reflection, you are already fulfilling your life's purpose, and you don't need to be confined to the walls of an office to achieve this. Instead of hurrying off to a scheduled meeting or office cubicle, cultivate an atmosphere of peace, rest, and thoughtful contemplation.

Your primary mission in life is to create something of significance, something that reflects your unique perspective and contribution to the world. Importantly, this act of creation is not restricted to conventional boundaries like an office desk; it can manifest anywhere, in any form, and at any time.

So, what exactly is it that you are creating? At the core, it begins with a thought. Every object, from the most rudimentary tool to the most sophisticated technological advancement, started as a fleeting idea within someone's mind. When you consider it, your very existence is the culmination of profound thoughts—those of your parents, who envisioned a life that eventually led to you. Thus, the thoughts we cultivate hold incredible power; they serve as the seeds from which all forms of creation germinate and grow.

Reflect on the intricate interplay between your thoughts, emotions, and actions. How you think directly influences your emotional state, shaping your words and actions. These actions eventually solidify into habits, eventually determining your success or failure in various endeavors.

We are inherently designed to think, which implies that we continuously generate positive or negative outcomes. When we nurture constructive thoughts, we lay the groundwork for remarkable accomplishments and breakthroughs. Conversely, toxic thoughts can plunge us into despair and impede our progress.

Your very first action each day should be to engage in the act of creation. Each morning, make it a priority to rise with intention and seek out a "power thought" that can guide your day. This guiding thought may present itself as a single, impactful word that resonates deeply with you; at other times, it may evolve into a more comprehensive and thoughtful sentence. Dive deep into these reflections, allowing your initial ideas to develop and mature into fully formed creative concepts.

Over the course of time, these "power thoughts" will become the sturdy foundation upon which all your pursuits stand, often yielding remarkable rewards that ripple through various aspects of your life.

Consider the myriad innovative inventions that have likely been lost in the shower's fleeting moments of solitude and reflection. There was a woman who shared a story about her great-grandfather—a visionary entrepreneur who experienced a stroke of divine inspiration that led him to conceive the idea of "moving stairs." Unfortunately, he chose not to act on that idea, and not long after, in 1892, Jesse Reno succeeded in patenting the idea for moving stairs, forever sealing his legacy.

Your foremost responsibility is to engage in profound thought and generate imaginative ideas. Creative inspiration is a universal gift; however, too many individuals become ensnared in the relentless pace of daily routines and obligations, neglecting to acknowledge the wealth of creativity within them. If we simply take the time to pause, reflect, and create, we can unlock extraordinary potential to tackle our personal dilemmas, address national challenges, and even confront global issues. The key lies in our willingness to allow ourselves the time and space to think deeply and innovatively.

Inquisitive Reflections

1. How can reframing our understanding of work impact our overall well-being and creativity?
2. What are some practical ways to cultivate an atmosphere of peace and contemplation in our daily lives?
3. In what ways can our thoughts influence our emotional state and subsequent actions?
4. Can you share an example of a personal "power thought" that has guided you in your daily routines?
5. Why is it important to prioritize moments of reflection and creativity over the demands of a busy schedule?
6. How can we overcome the challenges of toxic thoughts that hinder our creative potential?
7. What are some strategies for transforming initial thoughts into fully formed creative concepts?
8. How do the stories of innovators who failed to act on their ideas inspire us to take action on our own thoughts?

9. In what ways can embracing creativity on an individual level contribute to solving larger societal issues?

10. How can we encourage others to tap into their creativity and foster a mindset that values thoughtful reflection?

The Counterarguments

✓ What would you say to someone who argues that structured work environments are essential for productivity and creativity, providing crucial resources and collaboration opportunities?

✓ Have you considered that some individuals may thrive on routine and find inspiration in a traditional office setting?

✓ How would you address critics who claim that encouraging deep thought outside of a conventional workspace could lead to distractions and diminished accountability?

Action Steps

→ *Establish a Daily Reflection Routine:* Set aside dedicated time each day for deep thought and reflection. Whether it's in the morning or evening, create a quiet space where you can disconnect from distractions and engage with your thoughts. Use this time to explore ideas, set intentions, and cultivate a sense of peace.

↠ *Identify Your "Power Thought":* Each morning, choose a single word or phrase that resonates with you and serves as your guiding thought for the day. Write it down and keep it somewhere visible. Refer back to it throughout the day to align your actions and decisions with your intention.

↠ *Practice Mindfulness:* Incorporate mindfulness exercises into your daily routine. Techniques like meditation, deep breathing, or mindful walks can help you clear your mind, allowing for creative thoughts to emerge. This practice will enhance your ability to focus and promote a more open and imaginative mindset.

↠ *Document Your Ideas:* Keep a journal or digital document where you can write down your ideas as they come to you. Whether they are small thoughts or grand plans, capturing them helps you to refine and develop them over time. Review your notes regularly to identify patterns or concepts worth pursuing further.

↠ *Take Action on Your Ideas:* Select one idea from your reflections that you feel passionate about and take concrete steps to bring it to life

This could involve research, creating a prototype, or starting a conversation with others. Committing to action will transform your thoughts into tangible contributions, making your creative journey more fulfilling.

Strategy Two - Hover

The word "hover," more often than not, has a negative connotation, suggesting an overwhelming or excessive closeness to something— as if one is trying to control it. This concept can imply a sense of possessiveness and a deep consumption of that thought or idea. In this context, hovering means maintaining an intense focus, much like a laser beam that concentrates on a specific target with unwavering precision.

So, what is our first step?

When you receive a creative thought, your subsequent action should be to hover over it. Take the time to reflect: Is this a constructive thought that holds potential, or is it a toxic thought that could lead me astray?

I remember when I was newly married. There were times when my wife, Michele, would notice me sitting alone in a corner, curled up in a ball, seemingly lost in my own world. One day, she gathered the courage to ask me what I was doing, to which I replied, "I am working."

After spending years together, she later commented, "You are hovering over a thought, aren't you?" This question took me by surprise, and I inquired how she had come to that conclusion. She chuckled and said she could tell by the look on my face—the deep concentration—and the fact that she imagined she could see smoke coming out of my ears!

The reality is that most of us do not take the time to hover over our creative thoughts. Consequently, we often fall into the bad habit of allowing our thoughts to pass by without fully engaging with them. Have you ever had a moment where you felt a divine inspiration, perhaps a promising idea that seemed to come from a high power? Yet, almost instantaneously, you dismissed it with thoughts like, "Oh, come on, stop being so childish. This is foolish, and there's no way it could ever happen—not for someone like me." In that moment, you have effectively discarded the second Smart Work strategy and found yourself stuck in a monotonous grind where creativity seems stifled.

Adopting a productive pattern can make a significant difference: recognize a creative thought and then commit to hovering over it. Don't let it slip away too quickly. Embrace it. Take the time to sit with that thought—reflect on it, analyze it, and explore its implications— because this process is indeed work and is essential for growth.

Leadership expert John Maxwell offers a compelling philosophy regarding this approach. He uses a specific chair for this purpose, which he refers to as his "thinking chair." In a notable anecdote, a new employee who happened to be a close relative of the CEO observed an older man sitting quietly and staring out of the window in a nearby office each day. This new employee, suspicious of the man's apparent idleness, contemplated making a complaint to the boss. To his surprise, the response he received from the CEO was, "Don't you dare interrupt him. Last year, one of his ideas made us several million dollars." This highlights the importance of allowing space for thinking and reflection.

Further illustrating this issue, Microsoft conducted a study revealing that the average attention span of an adult is merely eight seconds, contrasted with a goldfish, which has a nine-second attention span. This stark comparison emphasizes how we have developed detrimental habits of lackluster focus and fleeting thoughts. However, the good news is that we have the capacity to change and grow.

We can practice hovering over our thoughts because this act is not only a form of engagement, but a fundamental aspect of productive work. We open the door to genuine creativity and innovation by nurturing our thoughts.

Inquisitive Reflections

1. What does the term "hover" imply when it comes to creative thoughts?
2. Why is it important to hover over a thought instead of dismissing it right away?
3. Can you share a personal experience where you had a creative thought that you initially dismissed? What was the outcome?
4. How does the story of John Maxwell and the "thinking chair" relate to the concept of hovering over thoughts?
5. What does the comparison of adult attention spans to that of a goldfish suggest about modern thinking habits?
6. In what ways can we practice hovering over our thoughts in our daily lives?
7. What benefits can come from nurturing and wrestling with a creative idea instead of letting it pass?
8. Why do you think many people struggle with maintaining focus on their thoughts?
9. How can the practice of hovering lead to personal or professional growth?
10. What strategies can you implement in your routine to improve your ability to hover over thoughts?

The Counterarguments

✓ What would you say to someone who argues that the fast-paced environment of modern life necessitates quick decision-making, making it impractical to hover over thoughts consistently?

✓ How would you address those who believe that hovering over thoughts may lead to overthinking and indecision, inhibiting rather than enhancing creativity?

✓ Have you considered the perspective that some people thrive on spontaneous inspiration and may find hovering counterproductive to their creative processes?

Action Steps

↠ *Create a Dedicated Space for Reflection:* Designate a specific area where you can sit quietly and think without distractions. This can be a comfortable chair, a cozy corner, or even a spot in nature. Use this space to focus on your thoughts and ideas.

↠ *Set Aside Time for Thought Engagement:* Schedule regular intervals in your day dedicated to thinking and reflection. During this time, allow yourself to explore your creative ideas without rushing. Treat it as a vital appointment for your mind.

↠ *Journaling for Clarity:* Write down your thoughts as they come to you. This practice not only helps you capture fleeting ideas but also allows you to process and reflect on them more deeply. Revisit your journal regularly to see how your ideas develop over time.

↠ *Ask Probing Questions:* When a thought arises, challenge yourself with questions like, "What potential does this idea hold?" or "What obstacles might it face?" This encourages deeper analysis and can unveil new perspectives on your creative thoughts.

↠ *Share and Discuss Ideas with Others:* Engage with trusted friends or colleagues about your thoughts. Sharing your ideas can bring fresh perspectives and constructive feedback that may enhance your initial concept, helping you to hover over it more effectively.

By incorporating these steps, you'll be better equipped to engage with your creative thoughts and to unlock your full potential.

Strategy Three – Speak Out

There is remarkable power inherent in our words.

My scientist friend introduced me to the groundbreaking work of Mr. Masaru Emoto, a Japanese researcher who in 1994 began an intriguing series of experiments involving water. Emoto would freeze water samples and meticulously photograph the unique crystals that formed. One particularly compelling study involved two separate containers of water. Over Container 1, he spoke words filled with positivity and encouragement, such as "love," "gratitude," and "peace." In stark contrast, Container 2 received negative, harsh words like "you are stupid" and "you are useless." The results were nothing short of astonishing. The water from Container 1 crystallized into stunning, intricate designs, exhibiting beauty and symmetry. Meanwhile, the water from Container 2 yielded amorphous, distorted crystals that lacked structure and grace. This striking contrast illustrates the tangible impact of positive and negative words.

Thoughts and Emotions

Leading neurologists affirm that each thought is accompanied by an associated emotion. This suggests that our words are not merely collections of sounds; they represent the work of our thoughts and feelings, carrying weight and influence in our lives and the lives of others.

To understand the depth of this concept, consider this progression:

- We think: Our thoughts are refined, intentional, and creative.
- We feel: Our emotions are deep and profound, reflecting our nature and character.
- We speak: We manifest our intentions and desires through our words.

One particularly fascinating scientific phenomenon is called sonoluminescence. This occurs when the sound waves in water create tiny bubbles that shrink and expand rapidly, releasing a brief burst of light. Given that the human body is composed of approximately 60 percent water, it's intriguing to consider that the sound of your words can generate light within you. This light symbolizes energy, force, and power, radiating outward and influencing everything around you. Your words are capable of bringing life, instilling hope, and facilitating transformation. May we be encouraged to harness this power.

One Man's Words

In the year 2001, I made the life-changing decision to move from South Africa to New Zealand. I took on a new job as a salesman selling home security alarms, filled with optimism for this new chapter. However, I quickly discovered that I was struggling to make sales.

The challenges mounted and, eventually, I faced eviction from the boarding house where I lived due to an inability to pay rent. My situation became increasingly precarious, ultimately resulting in my homelessness. During this difficult period, I found myself sleeping in the boardroom of the sales company where I worked.

One fateful day, while knocking on doors desperately trying to sell my product, I stumbled upon a public library. A sense of intuition urged me to step inside. While browsing the shelves, I discovered an audiocassette tape titled "See You at the "TOP" by Zig Ziglar. At that point, I had little money to spare, but I chose to rent that tape instead of spending it on lunch.

The moment I played that cassette, I was immediately captivated by the sound of Zig Ziglar's voice. It was filled with an electrifying energy, force, and unwavering conviction. His words stirred something deep within me, filling me with hope, inspiration, and excitement. It was as though the darkness surrounding my thoughts began to lift. Ziglar's message empowered me to believe in my potential and to aspire for greatness. The wisdom contained within his words illuminated my path and encouraged me to envision a brighter future. Carl W. Buechner's sentiment rings true: "They may forget what you said, but they will never forget how you made them feel."

The transformative experience of listening to Zig Ziglar's words marked a pivotal moment in my life. I distinctly remember pointing at the cassette player and proclaiming, "Mr. Ziglar, I do not know who you are, but this little broke salesman will one day stand on stages around the world and speak like you." I listened to that cassette hundreds of times, and through the inspiration I derived from it, I managed to turn my life around. I transitioned from being a struggling salesman to one of my company's top salespeople. My progress continued as I advanced to a sales manager role and later opened my own branch.

Seven years later, I found myself at a seminar in Dallas, Texas, where someone heard me share my story during a roundtable discussion. He encouraged me to speak from the platform to the entire audience, and to my surprise, Zig Ziglar was present that day. When I finished my talk, the vice president of Ziglar invited me to join the Ziglar family. This led to my certification as a speaker and trainer, and I ultimately moved to America. Today, I proudly hold the title of a Ziglar Platinum Speaker, fulfilling the dreams that were sparked by the power of spoken words.

Can you genuinely grasp the immense power behind your words? Your words carry the potential for life or death, light or darkness, victory or failure. Your words are your work; therefore, speak them with care and great purpose.

Inquisitive Reflections

1. What was the main experiment conducted by Masaru Emoto and what were its results?
2. How do thoughts and emotions relate to the power of our words?
3. Can you explain the concept of sonoluminescence and its connection to the impact of spoken words?
4. Describe the challenges the author faced after moving to New Zealand.
5. How did Zig Ziglar's audiocassette have a transformative effect on the author's life?
6. In what ways did the author's situation change after listening to Zig Ziglar's message?
7. What lesson can be drawn from Carl W. Buechner's quote about words and feelings?
8. How did the author's journey culminate in becoming a Ziglar Platinum Speaker?

The Counterarguments

What would you say to someone who argues that personal anecdotes, while inspiring, may not offer sufficient evidence to support the broader claim about the power of words?

✓ Have you considered the perspective that the impact of words may vary drastically based on individual circumstances and backgrounds?

✓ How would you address critics who claim that the scientific evidence behind the influence of words is still inconclusive and warrants further research?

Action Steps

→ *Practice Mindful Communication:* Start being conscious of the words you use in your daily conversations. Reflect on how your words might affect others emotionally. Aim to speak positively and encourage those around you.

→ *Set Daily Intentions:* Each morning, take a few minutes to set intentions for your day. Decide on positive affirmations or uplifting phrases you want to remind yourself of. Use these words throughout the day to guide your thoughts and actions.

→ *Create a Gratitude Journal:* Dedicate time each day to write down at least three things you're grateful for. This practice not only focuses your mind on the positive but also helps you articulate your appreciation for the good in your life, reinforcing positive thinking.

⇉ *Listen to Inspirational Content:* Like the impact Zig Ziglar had on my life, seek out motivational books, speeches, or podcasts. Make it a habit to listen to or read inspirational material regularly to uplift your mindset and inspire yourself to grow.

⇉ Share Your Story: Look for opportunities to share your experiences and the lessons you've learned with others. Whether through speaking engagements, writing, or informal conversations, sharing your journey can inspire and empower others to harness the power of their own words.

Strategy Four - Insight

Insight goes far beyond simply having a good vision; it encompasses a profound understanding of what is occurring.

When we analyze the term "insight," our initial understanding may lead us to interpret it as the ability to "see." However, it is far richer and carries deeper implications. We perceive time in three distinct dimensions—past, present, and future—however, insight can see all three dimensions simultaneously. It conveys not merely physical sight but a profound depth into reality imbued with intelligence and intuition. Insight perceives our creative thought's entire journey and destiny in a single moment.

Therefore, we must be mindful of our thoughts and their potential to manifest in our lives. The process of transforming thoughts into reality is a powerful one; it requires that our thoughts be set free from the confines of our minds to take form in the world around us. By employing insight, intelligence, and intuition, we can witness the realization of our thoughts, however impossible they may seem initially. It is essential that we grant our thoughts the freedom to develop into whatever is destined for them.

Reflecting on my own journey, I realize that I had a vision of becoming a public speaker years ago. One particular moment stands out: I was parked outside a playground, the low fuel light blinking ominously, and I was financially strained. As I listened to a Zig Ziglar cassette tape that I had rented, I was moved by his powerful closing message: "And I will see you at the TOP!" At that moment, I vividly imagined myself speaking at prestigious stages around the globe. I could hear the audience responding to me, feel their energy, and visualize myself connecting with them.

My insights allowed me to see my future, my intelligence shaped my articulation, and my intuition guided the expression of my emotions. Years later, that sight materialized into my reality, affirming the power of thought and belief.

The Wisdom of an Ant

More than 3,000 years ago, King Solomon—legendary for his unparalleled wisdom and vast wealth—profoundly stated, "Go to the ant, ... consider its ways, and be wise! It has no commander, no overseer or ruler, yet it stores its provisions in summer and gathers its food at harvest."

This observation is truly remarkable. Solomon took the time to observe the ant closely, challenging us to adopt this same level of curiosity and awareness in our own lives.

To cultivate our understanding and insight, let us examine the ant—a small yet extraordinary creature—and explore some of its fascinating behaviors from which we can derive wisdom. Notably, in the animal kingdom, ants are among the few species, alongside humans, that engage in farming their food. This unique trait signifies a remarkable level of foresight and planning.

Ants exemplify three vital characteristics through their actions:

1. Insight: Ants navigate their environment and make decisions based on an inherent understanding of their surroundings, often adapting their actions based on subtle changes.
2. Intelligence: They demonstrate problem-solving abilities, such as finding the shortest path to food

sources or working collaboratively to overcome obstacles.

3. Intuition: Ants possess an instinctive ability to sense danger and opportunities, guiding their movements and actions appropriately.

These three components—insight, intelligence, and intuition—work together as a powerful triad that empowers ants to thrive in their environments. Interestingly, many ant species have evolved to lack auditory and visual organs, meaning they cannot perceive the world in the same way that humans do. This limitation leads us to conclude that ants rely heavily on their innate abilities—insight, intuition, and intelligence—to navigate their lives successfully. Their exceptional capacity for insight enables them to thrive despite the absence of traditional sensory inputs.

It is important to emphasize that you do not need complete awareness of everything happening around you. In fact, sometimes having less input from the world can be liberating. Much of the world is filled with negativity and skepticism, but since ants are unable to see or hear this external criticism, they remain focused on their purpose.

Likewise, when you receive insight that prompts you to take action, it is crucial to ignore the negativity and disbelief of others who may tell you that you cannot achieve your goals.

What We Project

Ants have a unique ability to recognize both danger and opportunity. When they encounter these factors, they communicate via pheromones—chemicals that other ants can detect, signaling information about their surroundings. In a similar way, humans exhibit a form of "psychological projection." We project our feelings, attitudes, and beliefs into the world, which can help us open doors that we may have once thought were closed. This projection encapsulates our inner philosophies and beliefs, manifesting our essence without ever needing to speak a word. Therefore, it is vital to nurture a positive and constructive philosophy in life.

Your capacity to create a successful and fulfilling life relies significantly on your mindset rather than external circumstances, such as the economy. This highlights the importance of maintaining a perspective grounded in positivity and goodwill.

Make Thinking Your Work

Ants are engineered for victory. Remarkably, they are capable of lifting objects that are ten to fifty times their own weight, earning them the title of the strongest creatures relative to their size. They exhibit incredible speed and can chew at an astounding rate of 140 miles per hour. Some ant species have demonstrated the ability to lift up to one hundred times their own weight.

Similarly, humans possess the capability to achieve more than we often believe is possible. It is commonly understood that we only utilize about 10 percent of our cognitive potential. This reality suggests that we have the capacity to think more, think deeper, think longer, and think more creatively. I resonate with the British Special Air Service (SAS) motto: "Train Hard, Fight Easy." My personal philosophy is to "Think Deep, Work Light."

We inherently possess the ability to expand our thinking. Therefore, I encourage you to prioritize thoughtful contemplation. Invest time in thinking more deeply, for extended periods, and with broader perspectives. This intentional focus on improving your thinking is your essential work—adopt the mindset of the ant, and watch how your life can transform.

Inquisitive Reflections

1. What is meant by the term "insight," and how does it differ from simply having a vision?
2. How does insight allow us to perceive the past, present, and future simultaneously?
3. Why is it important to be mindful of our thoughts and their potential to manifest in our lives?

4. Can you describe a personal experience where your insight helped you achieve a goal or realize a vision?
5. What are the three vital characteristics exemplified by ants, as described in the text?
6. How do ants navigate their environment despite lacking traditional sensory inputs?
7. What lesson in terms of curiosity and awareness can we learn from King Solomon's observation of ants?
8. How do ants communicate danger and opportunity to one another, and what parallels can be drawn to human psychological projection?
9. Why is it essential to maintain a positive and constructive philosophy in the face of negativity?
10. In what ways can we cultivate the qualities of insight, intelligence, and intuition in our own lives?

The Counterarguments

✓ How would you address someone who argues that while insight is important, it can also lead to over-thinking, potentially paralyzing decision-making in moments that require quick action?
✓ What would you say to critics who claim that focusing too much on internal perceptions, like insight and intuition, can neglect the value of empirical evidence and analytical reasoning?

✓ Have you considered that some may argue that not all individuals have the same capacity for insight and that external support and guidance can be equally vital in helping people achieve their goals?

Action Steps

→ *Practice Mindfulness:* Take time each day to be present and aware of your thoughts and surroundings. Meditation, journaling, or simply spending quiet moments in nature can help you connect with your inner self and gain clarity.

→ *Reflect on Your Experiences:* Regularly analyze your past experiences and the insights you gained from them. Consider how your decisions shaped your current reality and how you can apply those lessons moving forward.

→ *Embrace Curiosity:* Adopt a mindset of curiosity akin to that of King Solomon observing the ant. Explore new ideas, ask questions, and seek to understand different perspectives. This can lead to valuable insights and innovative solutions.

→ Set Clear Intentions: Define your goals and visualizations with precision. Write down what you want to achieve and use techniques like vision boards to keep your aspirations in sight, allowing your thoughts to manifest into reality.

→→ Cultivate Positive Projection: Be mindful of the emotions and beliefs you project into the world. Foster a positive mindset and surround yourself with supportive influences, which can help you attract opportunities and overcome challenges.

By incorporating these action steps into your daily routine, you can enhance your capacity for insight and take actionable steps toward realizing your goals.

Strategy Five - Separate and Let Go

The experience of witnessing a space rocket launch is nothing short of exhilarating. As the rocket soars into the endless sky, reaching an altitude of approximately twenty-four nautical miles, an extraordinary event unfolds: the boosters, the powerhouse of the rocket, detach from the orbiter or external tank. This moment of separation is executed with meticulous precision; the boosters, having fulfilled their purpose, descend back to Earth, landing safely in the vast ocean below. Once retrieved, these boosters undergo a thorough refurbishment, transforming them back into reliable instruments of exploration, ready for future missions. This intricate process serves as a vivid illustration of the natural cycle of life and the critical importance of timely separation in achieving meaningful success. In a well-coordinated rocket launch, the moment of separation is crucial, ensuring that each component operates effectively, allowing the mission to advance.

The concept of separation mirrors the dynamics of our personal and professional lives in far-reaching ways. The act of discerning and separating various elements is indispensable for cultivating a victorious and fulfilling existence. We must engage in this practice with vigilance and intent; for instance, the pesky weeds must be diligently uprooted from grass, sheep must be clearly identified apart from the goats, and uplifting thoughts should be carefully sifted from the negative ones that weigh us down. Not every idea deserves our attention, and not all thoughts will yield fruitful results. The process of dividing and separating can often be painful and arduous, especially when it entails letting go of cherished individuals or long- held beliefs. Nonetheless, it is this essential work that fosters our personal growth and development. Embracing the responsibility of separation becomes a pivotal part of our journey toward a richer life.

As we navigate various projects or ventures, we inevitably encounter moments that call for decisive division and separation, where we must eliminate elements or individuals that no longer align with our aspirations. Clinging to relationships that hinder our progress can lead to stagnation, trapping us in cycles of negativity. In certain circumstances, this may even mean parting ways with clients who no longer resonate with our vision. Recognizing that holding onto even the right individuals at the wrong time can obstruct the opportunities that are in store for us is crucial. When we choose to surround ourselves with those who do not uplift or support us, we risk being burdened by their presence, dragging us down into unproductive endeavors. Thus, the practice of carefully evaluating our relationships and commitments is vital, ensuring our efforts remain fruitful and our paths forward are clear.

It is essential to understand that much of our hard work often stems from the presence of the wrong people in our lives, creating unnecessary challenges and obstacles.

Pruning

The metaphor of pruning plays a crucial role in nurturing a fruitful and prosperous life. Pruning refers to the intentional act of removing unproductive or unnecessary elements to encourage growth and renewal. Just as a gardener nurtures plants through careful pruning, we can foster our own development by eliminating what no longer serves us.

Consider, for instance, the story of a client I will refer to as John. John found himself entangled in a challenging predicament, locked in a non-compete contract with a business partner whose behavior was notoriously difficult. Despite the seemingly lucrative financial benefits of this partnership, the chaotic and stressful atmosphere it created turned John's daily life into a relentless nightmare. Over the course of five transformative years of coaching, every time John sought advice on his toxic business relationship, we consistently arrived at the same conclusion: he needed to extricate himself, cut his losses, and take the bold step of venturing out on his own. However, John found himself trapped in the dilemma of "freedom versus the unknown." The familiar pain of his current situation felt safer than the uncertainty that lay ahead, leaving him apprehensive about making a significant change.

Eventually, the time came when I had to step back from my coaching role with John. Though it was a heart-wrenching decision, it became essential for both of us to embrace growth. A few years later, I was overjoyed to receive an inspiring email from John, announcing that he had finally summoned the courage to pursue a new path. Today, John successfully leads his own thriving international business and has ascended to the role of a senior government official. Predictions abound that he may even become the president of his country, standing as a testament to the transformative power of making the right choices at the right moment.

The significance of the strategy of dividing and separating cannot be overstated. Everything in its natural state, if left unchecked, will inevitably break down, decay, and rot. The regenerative process of life compels us to cut off, prune, and remove elements that no longer serve a constructive purpose, allowing for new growth and possibilities to emerge. Even the most flourishing aspects of our lives require attention and care to ensure they continue to thrive.

Inquisitive Reflections

1. What is the main theme of Strategy Five – Separate and Let Go?
2. How does the rocket launch process illustrate the importance of timely separation in achieving success?
3. Why is it important to distinguish between different elements in our personal and professional lives?
4. What does the metaphor of pruning represent in the context of personal growth?
5. Can you summarize John's experience and the lessons he learned through his coaching journey?
6. How does the concept of separation relate to evaluating relationships and commitments?
7. What are some examples of situations where one might need to practice separation in their own life?
8. Why do you think people struggle with letting go of toxic relationships or unproductive commitments?

9. What role does fear of the unknown play in someone's decision- making process when considering separation?
10. How can individuals foster their own development by applying the principles of separation and pruning?

The Counterarguments

✓ How would you respond to someone who argues that the fear of the unknown may prevent individuals from recognizing the need for separation, leading to potential stagnation in their personal or professional lives?

✓ What would you say to a reader who suggests that not all relationships or ideas require pruning, and some may offer valuable lessons despite their challenges?

✓ Have you considered the perspective that the act of letting go can sometimes be seen as avoiding necessary conflicts or difficult conversations instead of truly fostering growth?

Action Steps

→ *Conduct a Relationship Audit*: Take time to evaluate your relationships, both personal and professional. Identify which connections uplift and inspire you and which ones drain your energy or hinder your progress. Create a list to visualize this and consider implementing changes where necessary.

→ *Set Clear Boundaries:* Learn to establish and communicate boundaries with individuals or commitments that do not align with your goals and values. This might involve having difficult conversations or declining opportunities that no longer serve your best interests.

→ *Reflect and Let Go:* Engage in regular self-reflection to identify beliefs, habits, or routines that may be holding you back. Allow yourself to let go of these limiting factors and focus on cultivating new, positive habits that encourage growth and renewal.

→ *Practice Mindful Decision-Making:* When faced with choices, take a moment to assess how each option aligns with your aspirations and overall well-being. Make decisions that promote clarity and growth, even if it means parting with what is familiar.

Strategy Six - Speak Out The Destiny

The labels we carry throughout our lives profoundly influence our sense of purpose and the direction we choose to pursue. The practice of naming, coupled with the significance underlying the names we are given, delves deeply into the fabric of our personal journeys, enriching us with layers of meaning. From the moment your parents select a name for you at birth, often imbued with the weight of family history, cultural heritage, or even the aspirations of those who came before you, this seemingly simple act creates a pivotal framework for your interactions with the world around you.

As we grow and develop, society begins to associate us with that name, which helps shape our external persona. This persona—crafted from the expectations of family, friends, and society—serves as the tangible face of our identity. It acts as a mirror reflecting not only how we are perceived, but also how we perceive ourselves in the context of those expectations.

However, beneath this outward label exists a deeper truth tied to our true identity: an understanding of the essence that embodies our divine purpose and unique potential. This internal essence transcends any name or title; it resonates as a powerful affirmation of who we are meant to be—an intimate declaration that encompasses our relationships, personal missions, and innate gifts. Ultimately, the names and titles we carry are not just identifiers; they play an instrumental role in forging the pathways of our lives, guiding us as we strive to discover and fulfill our unique vocations.

Our endeavors as individuals encompass much more than the mechanical execution of tasks or projects; they require us to articulate the very essence of these pursuits, nurture their development, and boldly proclaim their destined paths in the wider world. Life can be likened to a rich tapestry, woven with the stories of individuals who have embraced the power of renaming—be it themselves or others— thereby inviting those around them to engage with the fullness of their identities and destinies. When we articulate an idea or a project within the context of its intended purpose, we grant it both the permission and encouragement to thrive, pursue growth, and ultimately achieve lasting prosperity.

A poignant narrative serves to illustrate this concept compellingly: A prominent sportsman, seeking to inspire those in a challenging environment, shared his insights in a prison setting with a group of individuals grappling with the fallout of their choices. His keynote speech was titled "I Am What My Father Said I Would Be," and it drew deeply from his personal experiences. As he recounted the early years of his life, he vividly unveiled the significant moments when his father affectionately referred to him as "champ." This designation wasn't merely a casual endearment; it imbued him with an enduring sense of hope and aspiration for his future. His father consistently nurtured this belief, instilling in him the conviction that "One day, you will be a famous sportsman." He wove a positive vision of greatness into the very fabric of the young boy's identity, setting a lofty yet promising trajectory for his life.

After delivering his heartfelt address, he wandered through the stark prison corridors, where he encountered an inmate who captured his attention. Upon locking eyes with the player, the prisoner shared a striking sentiment: "Sir, I, too, am the man my father said I would become. My father called me 'convict' and grimly foretold that I would one day find myself behind bars." This powerful juxtaposition of their narratives starkly illustrates the impactful influence that the labels we receive from our parents and others exert over our destinies. It underscores the essential nature of affirmation and calling in shaping the journey of an individual, highlighting how deeply our identities can be affected by the words we hear in our formative years.

Moreover, the names we assign to our ventures—whether they are businesses, projects, or our own self-perceptions—carry immense weight, profoundly shaping how we choose to interact with our realities.

Mark Twain aptly reminds us of the dual significance of our existence when he stated, "The two most important days in a person's life are the day you are born and the day you find out why." The reverberation of these wise words emphasizes a profound truth: discovering our purpose represents a pivotal and transformative moment, echoing through the corridors of our lives.

Accurately naming our projects and recognizing their intended destinies extends beyond mere importance; it embodies a transformational endeavor. Each name transcends being a label; it becomes an affirmation of potential, a declaration of possibilities, and a destiny patiently waiting to be fulfilled. Thus, the act of naming emerges as a powerful instrument within our lives, shaping not only our perceptions but also the reality we aspire to create. By framing our endeavors with purpose and intent, we invite ourselves and others to join in the journey toward their greatest fulfillment.

Inquisitive Reflections

1. How do the names we receive at birth influence our identity and purpose throughout our lives?
2. In what ways does society shape our external persona based on the names we carry?
3. What is the distinction between our outward labels and our internal essence, and why is it significant?
4. Can you think of a personal example where a name or title you hold impacted your sense of self or your ambitions?
5. Why do you think it's important to articulate the essence of our pursuits and projects?
6. How does the story of the baseball player and the inmate highlight the concept of affirmation in shaping identity?
7. What role do names play in the success and perception of our ventures, such as businesses or personal projects?
8. How can accurately naming our endeavors transform how we interact with our goals and aspirations?
9. In what ways can we invite others to engage with our true identities and destinies through the act of naming?
10. Reflecting on Mark Twain's quote, how has discovering your purpose transformed your life?

The Counterarguments

✓ How would you address those who argue that the significance of personal labels may be overstated, as individuals often define their identity through experiences rather than names alone?

✓ What would you say to a reader who claims that not everyone has supportive or affirming figures in their lives, and that this can lead to to a divergent understanding of identity, regardless of naming?

✓ Have you considered the possibility that cultural variations in naming practices might lead to different perceptions of identity and purpose, challenging the universality of your argument?

Action Steps

↪ *Reflect on Personal Labels:* Take time to evaluate the names and labels you've been given throughout your life. Consider how these have shaped your identity and sense of purpose. Write down both positive and negative labels and contemplate their influence on your self-perception and aspirations.

↪ *Reframe Your Narrative:* Identify any limiting beliefs that have been reinforced by the labels you've received. Practice reframing these narratives into empowering affirmations. For example, if you've been labeled as "impractical," revise this to recognize your creativity and innovative thinking.

↠ *Set Intentional Goals:* Based on your reflections and reframed narrative, set specific goals that align with your true essence and desired life path. Ensure that these goals resonate with your passions and values, serving as stepping stones toward fulfilling your unique purpose.

↠ *Articulate Your Vision:* Create a clear and compelling mission statement for yourself, your projects, or your business. Define the purpose behind each venture and articulate how it aligns with your identity and aspirations. This will help in guiding your actions and attracting support from others.

↠ *Engage in Affirmative Naming:* When starting new projects, businesses, or even self-initiatives, choose names that reflect the positive potential and vision you want to embody. Share these names and their meanings with others to invite collaboration and support, fostering a community that believes in the journey towards fulfillment.

Strategy Seven - Made for Love

In our existence, we must recognize that we are not merely self-made individuals. Each man and woman is intricately woven into the fabric of creation through love. When you create something out of love— art, literature, or any form of expression—your unique personality and essence are evident in that creation. Similarly, every living creature around us—whether a towering tree, a delicate shrub, or a bustling animal—reflects an aspect of nature's love. Yet, what sets humanity apart is our being made for love. We are endowed with a passion and deep compassion that embodies our creativity.

Every creation is meant to showcase the personality and intentions of its maker. Therefore, every human being is a masterpiece, marked by infinite love. A passionate creator takes immense pleasure in their work, fashioning with purpose and care.

It's not about products or services or the transactional nature of the business; it is our creative power of love.

Each one of us is an extraordinary example of love's creative genius.

Understanding this truth—that we do not have to toil endlessly to create our own destinies—should inspire and uplift our spirits. Instead of laboriously striving to balance life's demands and challenges, we ought to acknowledge that many aspects of our lives can work out seamlessly through the force of love. We were not designed to struggle for more money, more work, or market share.

We were made for love, which empowers us to achieve remarkable accomplishments that transcend the limits of our human capabilities.

Our essential purpose lies in facilitating love and compassion within our lives and those around us. Embracing this calling might require significant sacrifice and a willingness to relinquish our agendas and desires. Allowing love to work through us requires more than a mere declaration of "I love what I do"; it demands a total commitment of our entire being—our intellect, passions, aspirations, and will. It is a conscious and deliberate sacrifice to relinquish our desires and say, "I will do everything out of love for others and myself."

Ultimately, this commitment is about presenting ourselves as living examples of doing good, affirming, "Today, I surrender my desire to work out of love and love will work through me. I will cease my internal struggles and embrace the truth that I am made for love."

Be Humble Before All

The virtue of humility is crucial to human relationships. I do not imply that you must be weak or lack self-worth. I refer, instead, to the heart posture of humility, which involves releasing inflated ego and pride that often obstruct our growth and hinder the flow of victory in our lives.

Pride acts as a substantial barrier, preventing goodness and greatness from reaching us and radiating through us to touch the lives of others.

When you actively choose to humble yourself before others, the power of love uplifts and elevates you in the eyes of others, establishing your good reputation. This concept may seem paradoxical, yet it underscores the path to genuine victory and fulfillment in life.

Amidst the myriad of identities and labels we might hold, I believe the most profound title we could ever claim is "I am made for love." This title encapsulates our intrinsic worth and identity as influential creators, constantly reminding us of the purpose and extraordinary potential that lies within each of us. Acknowledging this truth empowers us to live authentically and purposefully, fulfilling the unique roles we were designed to play in the grand tapestry of creation.

Inquisitive Reflections

1. What does it mean to say that we are "made for love"?
2. How do you think love influences creativity and expression in our lives?
3. In what ways can recognizing our interconnectedness improve our relationships with others?

4. Why is humility considered a crucial virtue in fostering strong human relationships?

5. How can we practically embody the idea of "doing everything out of love for others and myself"?

6. What are some sacrifices we might need to make in order to prioritize love in our lives?

7. How do pride and ego act as barriers to personal growth and the flow of goodness in our lives?

8. Can you think of a time when you experienced a situation where love led to a positive outcome, either for yourself or someone else?

9. What does living authentically and purposefully look like for you on a daily basis?

10. How can we remind ourselves of our identity as creators made for love amidst the challenges of everyday life?

Feel free to answer any or all of these questions!

The Counterarguments

✓ How would you respond to someone who argues that focusing solely on love might neglect the importance of personal responsibility and individual effort in achieving success?

✓ What would you say to critics who claim that love cannot be the sole motivator for creativity and that external factors also play a significant role?

✓ Have you considered the perspective that a mindset solely centered on love may overlook the complexity of human emotions and experiences, which can also include fear, ambition, and desire?

Action Steps

→ *Practice Mindfulness and Reflection:* Dedicate time each day to reflect on your intentions and actions. Consider how you can incorporate love into your daily tasks—whether at work, home, or in interactions with others. Journaling can be a powerful tool for this reflection.

→ *Engage in Acts of Kindness:* Make a conscious effort to perform small acts of kindness every day. This could be as simple as helping a neighbor, complimenting a colleague, or volunteering your time to help those in need. Each act reinforces your commitment to love and compassion.

→ *Cultivate Gratitude:* Begin and end your day by listing three things you are grateful for. This practice helps shift your focus away from struggles and towards the abundance in your life, fostering a mindset aligned with love and appreciation.

→ *Embrace Vulnerability:* Allow yourself to be open with others. Share your thoughts and feelings authentically and encourage those around you to do the same. This vulnerability fosters deeper connections and enhances mutual understanding.

→ *Develop a Humble Mindset:* Regularly remind yourself of the value of humility. Seek feedback from others, and be willing to learn and grow from it. Recognize that true strength comes from understanding and acknowledging the contributions of others rather than solely focusing on your accomplishments.

Implementing these steps can help you live more intentionally, reinforcing the love and compassion that define our existence.

Strategy Eight – Correct Positioning

Understanding where you should be, what you should do, and how you should do it is pivotal to realizing your purpose on earth. Proximity matters significantly in our journey. Often, we overlook crucial opportunities because we fail to recognize the correct positioning in our lives.

Great strategists know that cultivating the art of positioning is vital. They inquire about those who are open to their message, connect with them, and offer genuine friendship. This reflects a profound truth: our interactions and placements are intended to foster connections that can lead to mutual growth and understanding.

In the realm of real estate, achieving success hinges on "location, location, location!" Yet, when it comes to leading a life of purpose and impact, I propose a different mantra: "position, position, position!" Finding oneself in the right position leads to peace, prosperity, favor, and well-being—not just for ourselves, but for everyone around us. Correct positioning aligns us perfectly with our life's calling and mission, allowing victory and prosperity to unfold in our lives.

Reflecting on Personal Positioning

Looking back at my life, I can identify moments when I was undoubtedly correctly positioned at the right place and time. Each opportunity and connection felt like a vital link in a chain, intricately connecting individuals, moments, and victories. These moments often appear random, but they are anything but. They reveal the tapestry that weaves through each of our journeys.

A Life-Changing Bicycle Encounter

I recall when I was about fourteen, my mother noticed an old bicycle for sale for twenty-five dollars. However, she only had fifteen. Yet, she insisted, "There's a bicycle I want to buy for you. Let's go and see it." We walked to the seller's place, and when my mother offered her fifteen dollars, the seller seemed confused yet intrigued. And gave me the bicycle. That bicycle brought me joy for several years, and ultimately, I sold it to purchase an even better one.

An Unlikely Opportunity

One day, feeling led to venture into a predominantly "White village" during Apartheid South Africa, I encountered a group of men. As one of them approached me, I was a bit nervous because back in those times, there was so much racial hatred, and we were not welcomed in certain areas. But he asked if I would sell him my bicycle. I didn't hesitate to sell it as it felt like I had just received a million dollars, but more than that, I made a friend. For the first time in my youth, I realized there were good people in the world.

In the weeks that followed, I found myself standing outside a security training company, drawn by the prospect of signing up for a program that cost a hundred dollars. Shortly after, I turned eighteen and went out seeking employment. I hitched a ride into the city and walked several miles, knocking on doors, but received no offers. Exhausted and disheartened, I sat on the roadside.

A vehicle pulled up, and the driver asked what I was doing in such a dangerous area. I shared that I was searching for a security job. To my amazement, he revealed that he owned a security company, but was hesitant to hire me due to my lack of experience. However, upon hearing my name, he chuckled and said, "My name is Pillay too! Now I have to give you a job." And he did.

From Trials to Triumphs

I was assigned to a shopping mall, working the night shift alone. Though the job was risky, a restaurant manager took notice of me and kindly offered me food each night. He also encouraged me to seek better opportunities within the industry, even mentioning a relative who worked for a major security company. Eager to advance, I followed his advice— and it led me to a new job.

After completing my training, I earned certification as a supervisor in a large international company. However, the job took me far from home. Fortunately, my uncle lived nearby, and I was able to stay with him.

Each day, on my way to work, I passed by a hospital. One day, I noticed a familiar face—a man from my hometown. Our chance encounter led to an unexpected opportunity, as he helped me secure a job at the hospital.

Through this job, I met a woman who managed a food cart. She mentioned that her sister had a room for rent nearby, and I soon found myself settling into a new home. What seemed like a simple change led to unexpected yet beautiful turns in my life.

The homeowner had a nephew in New Zealand, and through that connection, I was inspired to travel there a few years later. It was during that visit that I discovered Zig Ziglar's tapes—a discovery that ignited my journey into the world of international speaking.

Today, I find fulfillment in advising high-impact businesses, a journey that has been woven together by correct positioning throughout my life. Each experience reaffirmed that our placement— whether for a brief season or an extended period—holds a purpose to revolutionize our lives and those around us. Trusting in correct positioning catalyzes profound transformations, reminding us of the incredible plans that have been laid out for each of us.

Inquisitive Reflections

1. What does the author mean by "positioning" in the context of achieving one's purpose in life?
2. How does the author's childhood experience with the bicycle illustrate the concept of correct positioning?
3. What key lesson does the author learn from the encounter in the predominantly "White village" during Apartheid South Africa?
4. How does the author's job search illustrate the idea of unforeseen opportunities arising from correct positioning?
5. In what ways does the author connect his experiences in the security industry to his current work advising high-impact businesses?
6. What role do personal connections play in the author's journey, as mentioned in the text?
7. How does the author define success in relationship to positioning compared to the common real estate mantra of "location, location, location"?
8. What transformations or opportunities does the author attribute to their correct positioning throughout life?
9. How can the concept of "position, position, position" apply to other areas of life beyond career and business?

10. What final thoughts does the author share about trusting in correct positioning and its impact on personal and collective growth?

The Counterarguments

✓ How would you respond to a reader who argues that personal effort and individual initiative, rather than positioning, play a more crucial role in achieving success and fulfillment in life?

✓ Have you considered the perspective that some opportunities may arise from chance encounters rather than being solely attributed to one's positioning?

✓ What would you say to someone who claims that one's environment and circumstances can limit the effectiveness of positioning, potentially undermining its impact on success?

Action Steps

→ *Assess Your Current Position:* Take time to evaluate where you are in your life—what opportunities and connections surround you. Reflect on your strengths, values, and passions to gain clarity on your purpose.

→ *Expand Your Network:* Actively seek out connections that resonate with your vision. Attend events, join groups, or engage in online communities where you can meet individuals who share similar interests and goals.

→ *Cultivate Meaningful Relationships:* Focus on building genuine friendships and professional relationships. Offer support, share knowledge, and be open to collaboration. The strength of your network can lead to new opportunities.

→ *Pursue Growth Opportunities:* Embrace opportunities that come your way, even if they seem challenging or outside your comfort zone. Invest in yourself through training, mentorship, or educational programs that align with your aspirations.

→ *Stay Open and Adaptable*: Remain flexible and open to change. Life's unexpected turns can lead you to the right position at the right time. Trust the process and be willing to adjust your path as new opportunities arise.

Strategy Nine - Being Enough

Achieving greatness is wonderful, but if you are not enough without the stuff and the titles, then you will never be enough with them.

Our primary focus should not solely be on our deeds or our worthiness regarding our actions, but rather on recognizing and accepting our intrinsic value and goodness as humans.

Throughout my experiences over the years, I have had the privilege of connecting with tens of thousands of individuals. A prevalent theme among most people is their struggle with self-worth; many carry a heavy burden of feeling they are never good enough. This sentiment is not limited to those who seem outwardly confident or achieve success. Indeed, individuals in high positions often wrestle with the same feelings of inadequacy, regardless of how much they accomplish or how much they give or serve. A large segment of the population spends their lives pursuing approval and validation from others.

Unfortunately, this relentless quest for external affirmation can lead to a profound sense of disappointment and despair, as the critical voices of others can deeply wound and demoralize them. When we chase the approval of others, we become entangled in a strenuous and often thankless effort, and we can never truly satisfy those expectations.

Be Diligent—Free of Shame

In the fading light of a setting sun, a wise old man sat patiently on a weathered bench, the years of his life etched into the deep creases of his face, each line telling tales of triumph and challenge. His eyes, a piercing shade of blue, sparkled with a mix of warmth and gravity as he turned to his eager young protégé, whose eyes gleamed with ambition and curiosity.

"Listen closely, my young friend," he began, his voice steady and deliberate, resonating with the weight of his many experiences. "Be steadfast and diligent in your efforts; let your commitment shine through, so that one day you may stand tall, recognized as a worthy worker among your peers. Approach each task with unyielding sincerity and courage. Handle the truths that come your way with the utmost care and precision, for in doing so, you will discover your own brilliance."

He paused, allowing the gravity of his words to sink in. "The gold you seek—success, recognition, perhaps even wealth—will come to you in time. But let me impart one vital truth, my son: if you define your worth solely by the gold you possess, you will find that no amount of it can fill the void within. Your true value lies not in riches, but in the integrity of your character and the effort you put forth in every endeavor. If you are not enough without the stuff, you will never be enough with it."

Being diligent does not necessitate hard, exhausting labor; rather, it calls for eagerness and the willingness to acknowledge our intrinsic worth.

In this light, we must come to a place where we comfortably affirm the following truths about ourselves:

1. I am inherently good enough and have been approved.
2. My identity defines who I am, not what I do, emphasizing that I am worthy of my calling and destiny.
3. I will not carry shame from my past, my failures, or my shortcomings, as they do not define me.
4. I will not withhold from affirming my desire to achieve great things.

I recall a significant encounter I had during lunch with a new friend. About halfway through our meal, I began to sense a powerful prompting, "Tell him he is a good man," emerging in my thoughts. Driven by this prompting, I said, "My friend, I feel to tell you that you are a good man."

To my surprise, he paused and looked rather uneasy, replying, "Well, I don't think my wife would agree with that."

A few moments later, that same prompting returned, urging me again to communicate that he was a good man. So, I reiterated, "My friend, I really sense to tell you again that you are a good man."

He stopped eating again, visibly uncomfortable, saying, "I still don't think my wife would agree."

As we continued our lunch, I felt that same urging for a third time: "Tell him he is a good man." With renewed determination, I said, "My friend, I believe you are a good man."

This time, I saw a profound change in him. Tears welled in his eyes, and he finally responded, "Melvin, I am a good man." With that acknowledgement, it was as if a heavy burden lifted from him. He began to open up about his life, sharing the fears, failures, and struggles he carried. He admitted that he had never felt truly good enough for leadership, feeling trapped by his past mistakes. After experiencing some breakthroughs, he devoted himself to serving others, striving to be the best leader possible. However, this relentless pursuit burdened him with guilt and shame whenever he stumbled or fell short, leading to a sense of rejection.

As we spoke, he experienced a pivotal, life-changing moment, breaking free from the shackles of his mindset.

Many individuals are in a similar situation as this friend of mine, caught in the exhausting struggle to prove themselves as perfect leaders. In contrast, those who have embraced their true identity enjoy the freedom of simply "being enough," regardless of failures.

Your purpose transcends the traditional notion of working tirelessly for approval; your true calling is to embrace your identity and healthy self-belief of "being enough."

Inquisitive Reflections

1. What does the author believe is the key to recognizing one's intrinsic value?

2. How does the wise old man's advice emphasize the importance of character over material success?

3. How did the author's words impact his lunch companion during their conversation?

4. In what ways does the text suggest that the pursuit of external validation can be detrimental to our self-worth?

5. According to the text, how can embracing one's true identity lead to greater freedom and fulfillment?

6. What lessons about leadership and self-acceptance can be drawn from the author's experience with his friend?

7. How does the narrative illustrate the contrast between diligence and the pressure to achieve perfection?

8. What are some of the affirmations that the author suggests we should embrace about ourselves?

THE SMART WORK MATRIX

9. How can understanding our worth separate from past failures change our approach to challenges?

10. What role does vulnerability play in the process of acknowledging and accepting one's self-worth?

The Counterarguments

- ✓ What would you say to someone who argues that striving for excellence and achievement is necessary for personal growth, regardless of intrinsic worth?
- ✓ Have you considered the perspective that external validation can sometimes serve as a valuable source of feedback and encouragement rather than being solely detrimental?
- ✓ How would you address critics who claim that individuals may lack direction and fulfillment in their lives without ambition and the pursuit of success?

Action Steps

- ➡ *Practice Self-Reflection:* Dedicate some time each day or week to reflect on your strengths, values, and the qualities that make you unique. Journaling can be a powerful tool for this, allowing you to articulate and reinforce your self-acceptance.
- ➡ *Affirmations:* Create a list of positive affirmations that resonate with you, such as "I am inherently

good enough" and "My identity is defined by who I am, not by what I do." Repeat these affirmations daily to help reinforce a healthy self-image and boost your confidence.

→ *Seek Meaningful Connections:* Engage with people who uplift and encourage you. Surround yourself with individuals who recognize and appreciate your worth, and who can support you on your journey to self-acceptance.

→ *Challenge Negative Thoughts:* When you catch yourself feeling inadequate or unworthy, challenge those thoughts. Ask yourself what evidence supports them and counter with positive evidence of your accomplishments and character.

→ *Embrace Imperfection:* Allow yourself to make mistakes and understand that perfection is not a prerequisite for worthiness. Celebrate your progress and view challenges as opportunities for growth rather than measures of your value.

By taking these steps, you can cultivate a deeper understanding of your intrinsic worth and find fulfillment beyond external validation.

Strategy Ten – Leading with Rest and Inner Peace

Realizing that inner peace is not a goal to be achieved, but a state we already possess, can significantly boost our confidence and interactions. This understanding empowers and emboldens our efforts.

In this context, inner peace refers to experiencing a significant increase in joy and tranquility. A notable narrative illustrates this concept: A young boy in a small town aspired for great success and dreams that soared high. While exploring the ruins of an old structure, he discovered an ancient proverb carved into the stone wall. The proverb conveyed a powerful message:

> *"Overflowing with joy and peace is the one who chooses to do right, even when surrounded by those who veer into wrongdoing."*

This saying highlights the value of integrity and virtue, encouraging individuals to resist the temptation of self-interest and engage in positive, uplifting interactions instead of negativity or slander. According to the proverb, a long and fulfilling life filled with profound connections and integrity awaits such individuals. Inspired by this wisdom, the young boy resolved to lead a life defined by kindness and virtuous actions.

Embracing a life of integrity and peace can lead to prosperity in all endeavors. However, three essential conditions must be recognized to embrace this peaceful existence fully:

1. *Discern the Counsel You Follow:* It is crucial to be discerning about the advice and teachings you accept. Following self-centered perspectives can lead to misguided actions characterized by selfishness, detracting from the path of righteousness.

2. *Choose Your Companions Wisely:* The people we surround ourselves with can significantly influence our character and direction. Associating with those who exhibit narcissistic traits can lead us away from our true purpose. It's crucial to choose companions who encourage moral behavior and align with our values, being cautious and discerning in our choices.

3. *Avoid Negative Influences:* Engaging with individuals who mock, slander, or gossip undermines personal well-being. Such negative behaviors can impact our lives and the lives of those around us. By distancing ourselves from such influences, we can maintain integrity and dedication to a peaceful existence.

Neglecting these essential conditions may steer individuals away from the path of joy and peacefulness, potentially leading to adverse mental and emotional stress.

The Importance of Rest

Many individuals often feel guilty when taking time to rest, mistakenly believing that they should always be engaged in work.

However, rest is a fundamental aspect of life that deserves recognition and appreciation. Rather than viewing rest merely as a reward for labor, it should be acknowledged as an essential component of a healthy lifestyle. Restful moments allow us to recharge our minds and bodies, enhancing our ability to approach work with greater creativity and engagement.

Moreover, rest and reflection play a critical role in the natural rhythm of life. These intentional pauses in our daily routines convey the necessity for reflection, rejuvenation, and reconnection with a sense of peace. Taking breaks from daily demands allows individuals to contemplate life's purpose and recharge spiritually and mentally.

In this context, rest encourages seeking tranquility in a fast-paced world and highlights the importance of finding moments of peace amid life's chaos. Ultimately, understanding that rest is crucial for our well-being allows us to create space for personal growth, reflection, and alignment with our life's purpose.

Embracing stillness can reveal true brilliance. Researchers and neuroscientists have discovered that when a person is at rest or experiencing boredom, the brain enters a state known as the default or resting state. In this state, the brain is actively solving problems, and the longer you stay in this reflective mode, the deeper your thoughts can go, ultimately leading to greater creativity. It's said that the average adult's attention span is about eight seconds, while a goldfish's is around nine seconds. This comparison highlights our diminishing ability to focus and think deeply. Why is this happening? Because we are constantly distracted by technology. While we may believe we can multitask, the reality is that we only switch our focus rapidly from one thing to another. To counteract this, it's essential to step away from our phones and computer screens and take a moment to think.

In the song "The Gambler," performed by Kenny Rogers, there is a remarkable strategy for tackling life's challenges. Imagine a gambler on a summer night, surrounded by darkness and boredom, who shares wisdom with Kenny Rogers. He advises that to navigate life's game, you must know when to hold your cards, when to fold, when to walk away, and when to run. Boredom can serve as a catalyst for developing insightful life strategies. This encapsulates the essence of creativity. There is nothing inherently wrong with doing nothing; in fact, many brilliant minds have been perceived as unexciting. They may seem quirky, but if you spend enough time with them, you'll discover that they often engage in mundane activities like sitting quietly and pondering or gazing out a window for hours.

Neuroscientist Dr. Nancy Andreasen studied the patterns of highly creative individuals such as Einstein, Mozart, and da Vinci. She found that they all made time for what she calls "free-floating periods of thought." In her book, *The Creating Brain*, she explains how this habit varies from one person to another. For example, Leonardo da Vinci would sit in front of a painting and think for hours, while Einstein preferred to drift aimlessly on a small boat he named the *Tinef*. He often had to be rescued because he enjoyed being on the water so much that he didn't want to leave, even when it posed difficulties. A friend of his noted that while many would find being stuck frustrating, for Einstein it was simply more time to think.

To further explore this idea, Dr. Andreasen conducted a brain- imaging study to observe brain activity during these "free-floating" periods. She found that, instead of being quiet, the brain is actively engaged, connecting thoughts and experiences during these times. She termed this state REST, which stands for "Random Episodic Silent Thinking." During REST, the brain utilizes its complex parts to gather information and make connections.

Many creative individuals share their own versions of REST. Designer Paula Scher often comes up with ideas while sitting in the back of a taxi and allowing her mind to wander. Songwriter Paul Simon would relax in the bathroom with the sound of running water, which helped inspire his imagination. During one of these moments, he wrote the famous line, "Hello darkness, my old friend," from "The Sound of Silence." Filmmaker Quentin Tarantino also finds creativity in the water; he has stated that when he floats in his pool, ideas come to him, prompting him to take notes for his work later.

This mindset isn't about escaping work; it's about learning to engage with it more effectively. Take the time to sit, reflect, and embrace boredom. By doing so, you'll tap into your brain's creative potential to address life's challenges.

Inquisitive Reflections

1. What does the phrase "inner peace is not a goal to be achieved" mean in the context of the text?
2. How does the ancient proverb discovered by the young boy contribute to the understanding of integrity and virtue?

3. What are the three essential conditions mentioned for embracing a peaceful existence?
4. Why is it important to discern the counsel you follow, and how can it impact your life choices?
5. In what ways can the people we surround ourselves with influence our character and direction?
6. How does the text describe the importance of rest in relation to mental and emotional well-being?
7. What are the benefits of taking intentional breaks from our daily routines?
8. How does the concept of the brain's default state relate to creativity?
9. What comparison is made between the attention span of adults and goldfish, and what implications does this have for our focus?
10. What lesson can be drawn from the song "The Gambler" regarding handling life's challenges?

The Counterarguments

✓ What would you say to someone who argues that the idea of rest as essential might be undermined by the increasing societal pressure to be constantly productive?

✓ Have you considered that some people may find their sense of peace and purpose through continuous engagement rather than taking breaks?

✓ How would you address critics suggesting that an excessive focus on rest could lead to procrastination and avoiding responsibilities?

Action Steps

→ *Educate on the Benefits of Rest:* Share research and insights that highlight the positive effects of rest on mental clarity, creativity, and overall productivity. Use examples from successful people who prioritize downtime.

→ *Implement Scheduled Downtime:* Encourage individuals to consciously schedule breaks and periods of rest into their daily routines. This could involve techniques like the Pomodoro Technique, which emphasizes short breaks to boost focus.

→ *Promote Mindfulness Practices:* Introduce activities such as meditation or deep breathing exercises. These practices can enhance relaxation and mental clarity, demonstrating that rest can be an active component of productivity.

→ *Build a Supportive Culture:* Create environments (at work or in personal circles) that value and respect rest. This may include policies that encourage taking time off, flexible work hours, and creating spaces for relaxation.

➨ *Address Cultural Perspectives:* Engage in discussions about the varied perceptions of rest across cultures. This helps open up a dialogue on how different backgrounds approach productivity and can lead to a more inclusive understanding of work-life balance.

CHAPTER FIVE

ENTER THE MATRIX

Everyone has a plan until they get punched in the face.
~Mike Tyson

In the movie *Rocky Balboa*, Rocky, the main character, says these powerful words:

> "The world ain't all sunshine and rainbows. It is a very mean and nasty place and it will beat you to your knees and keep you there permanently if you let it. You, me, or nobody is gonna hit as hard as life. But it ain't how hard you hit; it's about how hard you can get hit and keep moving forward. How much you can take, and keep moving forward. That's how winning is done. Now, if you know what you're worth, then go out and get what you're worth. But you gotta be willing to take the hit and not point fingers saying you ain't where you are because of him, or her, or anybody. Cowards do that, and that ain't you. You're better than that!"

No matter how careful we are while driving, it's inevitable that we will encounter a pothole that disrupts our wheel alignment, resulting in a rough ride. The solution is to have the car's wheels realigned.

Similarly, life can present unexpected challenges that can throw us off balance, leading to feelings of spiritual emptiness, restlessness, conflict, weakness, deflation, lack, and passiveness. The answer lies in realigning your life by engaging in The Smart Work Matrix Alignment, an intuitive and straightforward tool crafted to help you realign various aspects of your life. By guiding you through a process of reflection and refocusing, it allows you to assess your current state in each area and identify where adjustments are needed. It aims to bring clarity and balance to your life, empowering you to align your goals and actions with your deepest values and aspirations.

THE SMART WORK MATRIX ALIGNMENT

Spiritual Alignment begins with consciously centering one's life around a greater power, recognizing that something is transcendent beyond individual existence. This journey often involves deep self-reflection and an exploration of personal beliefs, leading individuals to understand the importance of connecting with a source greater than themselves. By cultivating this awareness, one can find purpose and meaning in their actions, guiding their decisions and interactions in a manner that is harmonious with their spiritual values. Embracing this higher perspective fosters a sense of fulfillment and interconnectedness with oneself and all living beings.

Realignment Reflections

1. What does it mean to have spiritual alignment, and why is it important?
2. How can self-reflection aid in one's journey towards understanding their spiritual beliefs?
3. What are some ways to connect with a greater power beyond oneself?
4. In what ways can recognizing a higher source influence daily decisions and interactions?
5. How does cultivating awareness of a transcendent power contribute to finding purpose in life?
6. What role does interconnectedness play in the pursuit of spiritual fulfillment?
7. Can you provide examples of practices or activities that help individuals align with their spiritual values?
8. How might one navigate doubts or challenges in their spiritual journey?
9. What benefits can arise from embracing a higher perspective in everyday life?
10. How do different cultures or religions interpret the concept of a greater power?

Action Steps

Here are some action steps to help you align spiritually:

→ *Self-Reflection:* Set aside time each day for introspection. Journaling can be a great way to explore your thoughts, feelings, and beliefs.

→ *Meditation:* Practice meditation to quiet your mind and connect with your deeper self. This can help you become more aware of the transcendent aspects of life.

→ *Explore Personal Beliefs:* Take time to read, study, or engage in discussions about deeper spiritual beliefs. Consider what resonates with you and what doesn't.

→ *Set Intentions:* Define your spiritual values and what you want to achieve in your life. Write down specific goals that align with those values.

→ *Continuous Learning:* Commit to lifelong learning about spirituality, philosophy, and personal development to deepen your understanding and grow in alignment with your beliefs.

By following these steps, you can foster a deeper connection to your spiritual alignment and enhance your sense of purpose.

Mental Rest refers to our capacity to recognize and manage thoughts that create mental unrest. This mental disarray can lead to significant chaos in our lives, negatively impacting our overall well-being. When our minds are cluttered with stress, anxiety, or repetitive thoughts, it becomes increasingly difficult to achieve emotional and physical relaxation. This inability to rest can extend beyond mental fatigue, interfering with our daily functioning and negatively affecting our mood, focus, and productivity. By cultivating mental rest, we can learn to identify these disruptive thoughts and develop strategies to quiet our minds, ultimately allowing for a more restful and balanced state of being.

Realignment Reflections

1. What are some common signs that indicate a need for mental rest?
2. How can mental unrest impact our physical health?
3. What strategies can be implemented to cultivate mental rest?
4. Can mindfulness or meditation techniques assist in achieving mental rest? If so, how?
5. How does mental rest contribute to improved productivity and focus?
6. Are there specific practices for managing repetitive thoughts that disrupt mental peace?
7. In what ways can stress and anxiety hinder emotional relaxation?

8. How can one recognize when their thoughts are leading to mental chaos?

9. What role does self-awareness play in achieving mental rest?

10. How can mental rest be integrated into a daily routine?

Action Steps

Here are some actionable steps to cultivate mental rest:

- ✓ *Practice Mindfulness:* Set aside a few minutes each day to focus on your breath and observe your thoughts without judgment. This can help bring awareness to mental clutter.

- ✓ *Identify Triggers:* Keep a journal to note when you feel overwhelmed. Understanding the situations or thoughts that trigger mental unrest can help you address them more effectively.

- ✓ *Set Boundaries:* Learn to say no to commitments that drain your energy. Protect your time to allow for mental downtime.

- ✓ *Limit Screen Time:* Reduce exposure to social media and news, especially before bedtime. This can help prevent the overload of information and anxiety.

- ✓ *Engage in Physical Activity:* Regular exercise can significantly improve mental clarity and reduce stress. Find activities you enjoy to make it a consistent part of your routine.

✓ *Establish a Relaxing Evening Routine:* Wind down each night with calming activities such as reading or deep breathing exercises to prepare your mind for rest.

✓ *Limit Multitasking:* Focus on one task at a time to enhance concentration and reduce feelings of being overwhelmed.

✓ *Seek Support:* Talk to friends, family, or a mental health professional about your feelings. Sharing your thoughts can provide relief and new perspectives.

By implementing these steps gradually, you'll likely find it easier to quiet your mind and achieve a sense of mental rest.

Inner Peace involves recognizing and overcoming our instinctual tendency to seek control in various aspects of our lives. This journey requires us to confront the detrimental habit of worry, which often consumes our thoughts and leads to unnecessary stress. Additionally, we must let go of the unrealistic desire to fix every problem or challenge we encounter. By shifting our mindset and accepting that not everything is within our control, we can cultivate a sense of tranquility and acceptance, allowing us to navigate life's uncertainties with greater ease and resilience. Embracing this perspective fosters a profound inner calm, enabling us to live more fully in the present moment.

Realignment Reflections

1. What are some common ways we seek control in our lives, and how do these behaviors impact our mental well-being?
2. Why do you think worrying becomes a habit for many people, and what strategies can help break this cycle?
3. How can we differentiate between problems we can solve and those we need to accept as they are?
4. What practical steps can we take to shift our mindset toward acceptance and tranquility?
5. In what ways does embracing uncertainty contribute to greater resilience in our lives?
6. How can living in the present moment enhance our overall quality of life?
7. Can you share a personal experience where letting go of control led to a more peaceful outcome?

Action Steps

Here are some actionable steps to cultivate inner peace and shift your mindset:

- ✓ *Connect with Nature:* Spend time outdoors to foster a sense of connectedness with all living beings. Nature can be a powerful reminder of a greater power.

✓ *Limit News Consumption:* Reduce the amount of news you consume, especially if it causes anxiety. Stay informed but set boundaries around how frequently you check news sources.

✓ *Embrace Imperfection:* Accept that it's okay not to have solutions for every problem. Practice being comfortable with uncertainty and recognize that challenges are a part of life.

✓ *Gratitude Practice:* Each day, list three things you are grateful for. This simple practice shifts focus from worries to the positive aspects of your life.

✓ *Develop Healthy Coping Mechanisms:* Identify activities that help you relax, such as reading or art. Engage in these activities regularly to manage stress.

✓ *Deep Breathing Exercises:* Practice deep breathing techniques to calm your nervous system and reduce anxiety in stressful moments.

By incorporating these steps into your daily routine, you can gradually cultivate inner peace and resilience in the face of life's challenges.

Superpower embodies our inherent ability to harness and celebrate our unique gifts, talents, and abilities without fear or shame. It signifies the freedom to express ourselves fully and to share our strengths in ways that contribute positively to our own lives and the lives of others. This concept encourages us to recognize and utilize our capabilities for personal gain and the betterment of the community around us. By embracing our superpowers, we empower ourselves, inspire those around us, and create a ripple effect of positive change. Ultimately, it's about using our innate talents to uplift ourselves and others, fostering an environment where everyone can thrive and flourish together.

Realignment Reflections

1. What does it mean to harness our unique gifts and talents?
2. How can we express ourselves fully without fear or shame?
3. In what ways can recognizing our capabilities lead to personal growth?
4. How does embracing our superpowers influence the community around us?
5. Can you provide examples of how someone might use their unique talents to uplift others?
6. What are some challenges people face when trying to celebrate their superpowers?

7. How can we create an environment that encourages everyone to thrive together?
8. In what ways can we inspire others by sharing our strengths?
9. How does the concept of superpower relate to personal and professional success?
10. What steps can individuals take to discover and embrace their own superpowers?

Action Steps

✓ *Self-Reflection:* Take time to identify your unique gifts, talents, and abilities. Write them down and reflect on how they contribute to your life and the lives of others.

✓ *Set Intentions:* Clearly define how you want to use your superpowers. Set specific goals that align with your strengths and the positive impact you wish to create in your community.

✓ *Practice Self-Expression:* Find ways to express your talents, whether through art, volunteering, mentoring, or sharing your skills with others. This could involve joining local groups or online communities that align with your interests.

✓ *Embrace Learning:* Continuously seek opportunities to learn and grow. Take courses, attend workshops, or read books that help you develop your skills further.

✓ *Surround Yourself with Support:* Connect with like-minded individuals who celebrate their superpowers. Build a community that encourages and inspires you to shine.

✓ *Share Your Journey:* Document and share your experiences of embracing your superpowers. This could be through social media, blogs, or speaking engagements to inspire others.

✓ *Be Open to Feedback:* Seek input from others about your strengths and areas for improvement. Use this feedback to grow and refine how you express your superpowers.

✓ *Encourage Others:* Foster a positive environment by recognizing and celebrating the talents of those around you. Encourage them to embrace their superpowers and contribute to their growth.

✓ *Take Action:* Start small by taking daily actions that align with your strengths. Each step can lead to greater confidence and a larger impact.

By following these steps, you can fully embrace your superpowers and create positive change in your life and the lives of others around you.

Exercising Authority is fundamentally about harnessing our inner strength and self-discipline to manage our thoughts, emotions, and actions, particularly in challenging situations that may seem out of our control. It involves understanding that while we may not be able to change our circumstances, we can control our reactions and the choices we make in response to those circumstances.

This concept emphasizes the importance of self-awareness— recognizing our feelings and thought patterns—is a key first step in exerting authority over ourselves. By being mindful of our emotions, we can prevent them from dictating our actions, allowing us to respond thoughtfully instead of reactively.

Additionally, exercising authority encompasses setting personal boundaries and making deliberate decisions aligned with our values and goals. It's about taking responsibility for our lives, acknowledging that we can shape our experiences through our responses.

Realignment Reflections

1. What does exercising authority mean in the context of personal development?
2. How can self-awareness contribute to better management of thoughts and emotions during challenging situations?

3. In what ways can setting personal boundaries impact our ability to exert authority over ourselves?

4. Can you provide examples of how to respond thoughtfully rather than reactively in a stressful situation?

5. How does understanding our values and goals play a role in making deliberate decisions?

6. Why is taking responsibility for our lives important in the process of exercising authority?

7. What strategies can be used to improve self-discipline and inner strength?

8. How can we practice mindfulness to enhance our emotional regulation?

9. What are some common challenges people face when exercising authority over themselves?

10. How does exercising authority affect our relationships with others?

Action Steps

✓ *Identify Triggers:* Pay attention to situations or environments that trigger strong emotional reactions. Recognizing these triggers can help you prepare for them in the future.

✓ *Pause Before Reacting:* When faced with a challenging situation, take a moment to breathe and assess your feelings before responding. This pause can prevent knee-jerk reactions.

✓ *Set Clear Boundaries:* Define what is acceptable and unacceptable for you in various areas of your life (work, relationships, personal time) and communicate these boundaries to others.

✓ *Align Actions with Values:* Reflect on your personal values and ensure your daily actions and decisions are aligned with them. Create a list of values that are important to you.

✓ *Make Deliberate Choices:* Before making decisions, ask yourself how each choice aligns with your long-term goals and values. Take time to weigh the pros and cons.

✓ *Accept Responsibility:* Acknowledge your role in various outcomes in your life. Understand that while you can't control everything, you can control your reactions and decisions.

✓ *Seek Support:* Surround yourself with a supportive community or mentor who can guide and help you stay accountable in your self- management journey.

✓ *Evaluate Progress:* Regularly assess your ability to manage your thoughts, emotions, and actions. Reflect on your successes and areas for improvement.

By implementing these action steps, you can effectively exercise authority in your life, enhancing your ability to handle challenges and make thoughtful decisions aligned with your values.

Living Prosperously is a testament to our accomplishments in cultivating a rich, robust, and wholesome lifestyle. It goes beyond mere financial success; it encompasses our overall well-being and fulfillment in life. When individuals gaze into the mirror, they not only see their reflection but also recognize their intrinsic worth. They affirm to themselves, "I am valuable and worthy of investment, not just in material terms but in my growth, happiness, and self-care." This self-recognition is the foundation of a life where one truly understands the importance of nurturing their physical, emotional, and mental health, leading to a more enriching and satisfying existence.

Realignment Reflections

1. What does living prosperously mean to you?
2. In what ways can one cultivate a wholesome lifestyle beyond financial success?
3. How can individuals enhance their overall well-being and fulfillment in life?
4. What practices can help someone recognize their intrinsic worth?
5. Why is it important to invest in personal growth, happiness, and self-care?

6. How do physical, emotional, and mental health contribute to a satisfying existence?
7. What role does self-recognition play in achieving a fulfilling life?
8. Can you provide examples of nurturing activities for overall well- being?
9. How might societal pressures influence one's perception of worth and success?
10. What steps can someone take to start on a journey toward living prosperously?

Action Steps

✓ *Set Clear Goals:* Define what prosperity means to you beyond financial success. Consider aspects like health, relationships, personal growth, and fulfillment.

✓ *Invest in Self-Care:* Create a self-care routine that prioritizes your physical, emotional, and mental health. This could include exercise, meditation, reading, or spending time in nature.

✓ *Cultivate Gratitude:* Regularly acknowledge and appreciate the positive aspects of your life. This can enhance your overall well- being and shift your focus toward abundance.

✓ *Seek Personal Growth:* Commit to lifelong learning through courses, workshops, or new hobbies that foster personal development and enrich your life.

✓ *Build Supportive Relationships:* Surround your-self with people who uplift and inspire you. Nurture these relationships to enhance your emotional well-being.

✓ *Financial Awareness:* While it's important to look beyond material wealth, maintain awareness and understanding of your financial situation to ensure it supports your overall goals.

✓ *Balance Work and Play:* Make sure to allocate time for leisure and activities that bring joy and relaxation, fostering a sense of fulfillment.

✓ *Celebrate Your Achievements:* Acknowledge and celebrate your successes, no matter how small, to reinforce your sense of worth and motivation for growth.

Leading Victoriously signifies a profound transformation in our mindset and approach to life. It represents the ability to conquer the fears that often hold us back—fear of failure, which can para-lyze our ambitions; fear of rejection, which can stifle our authentic selves; and fear of judgment, which can inhibit our ability to express who we truly are.

In this state of being, we shed our timidity and passivity, choosing instead to embrace boldness and courage. It is a com-mitment to stepping outside of our comfort zones and facing challenges head-on, no longer allowing doubts or negative perceptions to dictate our actions or self-worth.

Moreover, Leading Victoriously is rooted in a strong foundation of Spiritual Alignment. This means connecting deeply with our values and purpose, allowing us to navigate through life with clarity and intention. Mental rest is essential as well; it fosters clarity of thought and resilience against the chaos of daily stress. Inner peace becomes our sanctuary, where we cultivate a sense of calm and stability, regardless of external circumstances.

Importantly, we embrace our Superpower—our unique strengths and talents—without guilt. We recognize that these gifts are meant to be shared, and we have the confidence to exercise our authority in various aspects of life, be it personal, professional, or social.

This empowerment allows us to live genuinely and prosperously, making choices that reflect our true selves and contribute to our overall well-being.

Ultimately, Leading Victoriously is about flourishing in all areas of our lives, with a profound sense of fulfillment and purpose, knowing that we have the ability to shape our destinies and make a meaningful impact on the world around us.

Realignment Reflections

1. What does "Leading Victoriously" mean to you personally, and how do you feel it could apply to your life?

2. Can you identify specific fears that have held you back in the past? How do you plan to confront them moving forward?

3. What strategies do you use to connect with your values and purpose?

4. How do you cultivate mental rest and inner peace in your daily life?

5. What unique strengths or talents do you believe are your superpowers, and how do you currently use them?

6. In what ways do you think sharing your gifts with others can enhance your sense of fulfillment and purpose?

7. Can you think of a challenge you've faced that you approached with courage? What was the outcome?

8. How can you cultivate a mindset that embraces boldness over timidity in your personal and professional life?

9. What areas of your life would you like to improve in order to lead more victoriously?

10. How do you define success, and how does "Leading Victoriously" fit into that definition?

Action Steps

- ✓ *Identify Your Fears:* Take time to reflect on what fears are holding you back. Write them down and acknowledge their impact on your life.
- ✓ *Set Clear Intentions:* Define what "Leading Victoriously" looks like for you. Set specific, achievable goals that align with your values and purpose.
- ✓ *Embrace Boldness:* Commit to tackling one fear at a time. Start small by stepping out of your comfort zone in daily situations, gradually building your confidence.
- ✓ *Celebrate Small Wins:* Acknowledge your achievements, no matter how small. Celebrating your progress reinforces positive behavior and motivates you to keep pushing forward.
- ✓ *Stay Resilient:* Develop coping strategies to handle stress and setbacks. Recognize that challenges are part of the journey and can be valuable learning experiences.

By following these steps, you can work towards leading victoriously, transforming your mindset, and ultimately embracing a life filled with purpose and fulfillment.

CHAPTER SIX

FREEDOM SEVEN

Your brain was wired for love; you were wired for love.

- Dr Caroline Leaf, Cognitive Neuroscientist

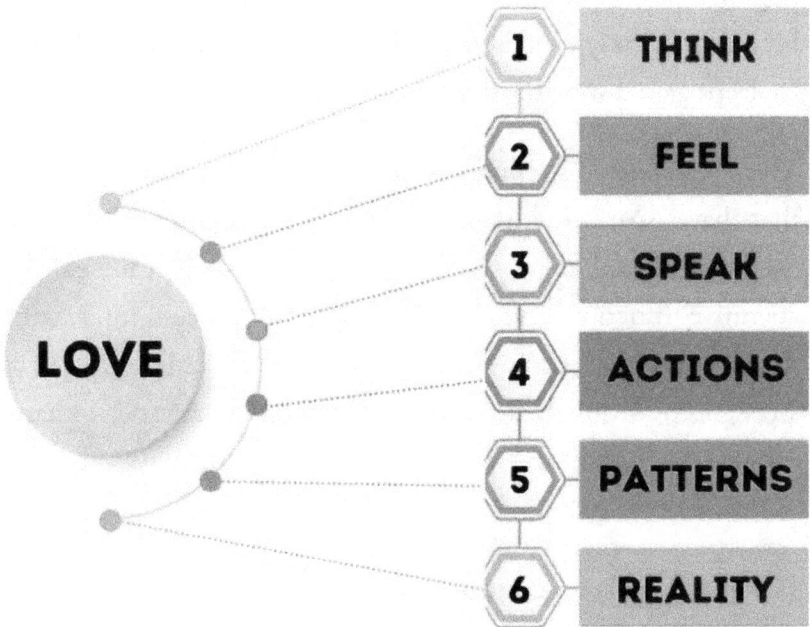

Free Your Mind and Live in Freedom

In the early 1990s, historian Roger Ekirch made a fascinating discovery about pre-Industrial sleep patterns, revealing that our ancestors engaged in a practice known as segmented sleep. This biphasic sleep model involved dividing the night into two distinct phases. In the first part, after sunset, individuals would go to bed and fall into a deep sleep for several hours. They would then awaken in the early hours of the morning, engaging in various activities ranging from work to personal pursuits or simple contemplation. This period of wakefulness lasted for a couple of hours before they returned to bed, often to sleep again during the daytime.

This segmented sleeping pattern had numerous advantages that have sparked renewed interest in its potential benefits. Studies suggest that practicing biphasic sleep can enhance cognitive function, allowing the mind to process information more effectively. Additionally, it can lead to reduced levels of stress, as individuals are afforded time to relax and recharge, ultimately resulting in increased productivity through-out the day.

Historically, many great minds have embraced unique sleep-ing practices to maximize their creative output. One notable example is Leonardo da Vinci, who is often credited with developing what is now referred to as polyphasic sleep. His method involved taking short naps of approximately 20 minutes, famously known as the power nap, which he utilized to extend his waking hours while maintaining high levels of mental clarity and focus.

Sleep is not merely a biological necessity; it is a precious gift that enhances our well-being and productivity. Embracing and prioritizing rest can lead to profound benefits for both the body and the mind. Instead of resisting the call of sleep, we should celebrate and enjoy it as a vital component of a healthy and balanced life.

We can break free from the system that has turned us into CEO slaves, employee slaves, self-employed slaves, and societal slaves. We open ourselves to freedom when we focus our minds and clear the clutter from our thoughts. Neurologists inform us that what we do within the first thirty minutes of waking each morning influences the rest of our day and establishes enduring habits. As noted, significant thoughts can be cultivated in as little as seven minutes. The encouraging news is that seven minutes a day for seven days can lead to meaningful changes in your thinking patterns and improve your mindset.

The wise King Solomon said that as a person thinks, so shall he or she be.

The way we think truly determines whether we lead a life along the path of most resistance or the path of least resistance.

Thankfully, we do not have to live a life that is always difficult, filled with overwork, stress, and worry. We can choose to think differently, knowing that if we are willing to change our thoughts, we can change everything.

Change is uncomfortable because of the many habits and patterns that have formed over the years. Most people find it hard to change, but with the right attitude and following this simple yet effective daily exercise, you can change your life and bring yourself freedom. It will help you think the right way, feel the right way, speak the right way, act the right way, form the right patterns, and live the right reality quickly.

The secret is capturing your "first" thoughts when you wake up. These thoughts are powerful because they dominate your day. They are very often mediocre, negative, or fleeting. Replace these thoughts with Power Thoughts.

There are 7 exercises. Complete one each day. When you wake up, read this chapter and follow the simple daily exercises for the day you are on.

Day 1: Power Thought LOVE

Step one: Say aloud,

Today, I will think about LOVE

Today, I will feel LOVE

Today, I will speak LOVE

Today, I will act with LOVE

Today, I will form patterns of LOVE

Today, I will live in the reality of LOVE

Step two: Think deeply about this thought for 60 seconds in a quiet, relaxed setting. Simultaneously, with your eyes closed, take a deep breath and exhale slowly. Do this seven times.

Step three: Embrace positive feelings and let them flow freely through you.

Step four: Write down the positive thoughts and feelings.

_____

_____

_____

_____

_____

Step five: Speak out the positive thoughts and feelings.

Step six: Take a 20-minute guilt-free, stress-free, and worry-free power nap, preferably in the afternoon, around 1-3 p.m.

Step seven: Identify the experiences contributing to your empowerment today or your future growth.

Day 2: Power Thought JOY

Step one: Say aloud,

Today, I will think about JOY

Today, I will feel JOY

Today, I will speak JOY

Today, I will act with JOY

Today, I will form patterns of JOY

Today, I will live in the reality of JOY

Step two: Think deeply about this thought for 60 seconds in a quiet, relaxed setting. Simultaneously, with your eyes closed, take a deep breath and exhale slowly. Do this seven times.

Step three: Embrace positive feelings and let them flow freely through you.

Step four: Write down the positive thoughts and feelings.

_____

_____

_____

_____

_____

Step five: Speak out the positive thoughts and feelings.

Step six: Take a 20-minute guilt-free, stress-free, and worry-free power nap, preferably in the afternoon, around 1-3 p.m.

Step seven: Identify the experiences contributing to your empowerment today or your future growth.

Day 3: *Power Thought PEACE*

Step one: Say aloud,

Today, I will think about PEACE

Today, I will feel PEACE

Today, I will speak PEACE

Today, I will act with PEACE

Today, I will form patterns of PEACE

Today, I will live in the reality of PEACE

Step two: Think deeply about this thought for 60 seconds in a quiet, relaxed setting. Simultaneously, with your eyes closed, take a deep breath and exhale slowly. Do this seven times.

Step three: Embrace positive feelings and let them flow freely through you.

Step four: Write down the positive thoughts and feelings.

_____

_____

_____

_____

_____

Step five: Speak out the positive thoughts and feelings.

Step six: Take a 20-minute guilt-free, stress-free, and worry-free power nap, preferably in the afternoon, around 1-3 p.m.

Step seven: Identify the experiences contributing to your empowerment today or your future growth.

Day 4: Power Thought PATIENCE

Step one: Say aloud,

Today, I will think about PATIENCE

Today, I will feel PATIENCE

Today, I will speak PATIENCE

Today, I will act with PATIENCE

Today, I will form patterns of PATIENCE

Today, I will live in the reality of PATIENCE

Step two: Think deeply about this thought for 60 seconds in a quiet, relaxed setting. Simultaneously, with your eyes closed, take a deep breath and exhale slowly. Do this seven times.

Step three: Embrace positive feelings and let them flow freely through you.

Step four: Write down the positive thoughts and feelings.

_____

_____

_____

_____

_____

Step five: Speak out the positive thoughts and feelings.

Step six: Take a 20-minute guilt-free, stress-free, and worry-free power nap, preferably in the afternoon, around 1-3 p.m.

Step seven: Identify the experiences contributing to your empowerment today or your future growth.

Day 5: Power Thought KINDNESS

Step one: Say aloud,

Today, I will think about KINDNESS

Today, I will feel KINDNESS

Today, I will speak KINDNESS

Today, I will act with KINDNESS

Today, I will form patterns of KINDNESS

Today, I will live in the reality of KINDNESS

Step two: Think deeply about this thought for 60 seconds in a quiet, relaxed setting. Simultaneously, with your eyes closed, take a deep breath and exhale slowly. Do this seven times.

Step three: Embrace positive feelings and let them flow freely through you.

Step four: Write down the positive thoughts and feelings.

_____

_____

_____

_____

_____

Step five: Speak out the positive thoughts and feelings.

Step six: Take a 20-minute guilt-free, stress-free, and worry-free power nap, preferably in the afternoon, around 1-3 p.m.

Step seven: Identify the experiences contributing to your empowerment today or your future growth.

Day 6: Power Thought GOODNESS

Step one: Say aloud,

Today, I will think about GOODNESS

Today, I will feel GOODNESS

Today, I will speak GOODNESS

Today, I will act with GOODNESS

Today, I will form patterns of GOODNESS

Today, I will live in the reality of GOODNESS

Step two: Think deeply about this thought for 60 seconds in a quiet, relaxed setting. Simultaneously, with your eyes closed, take a deep breath and exhale slowly. Do this seven times.

Step three: Embrace positive feelings and let them flow freely through you.

Step four: Write down the positive thoughts and feelings.

_____

_____

_____

_____

_____

Step five: Speak out the positive thoughts and feelings.

Step six: Take a 20-minute guilt-free, stress-free, and worry-free power nap, preferably in the afternoon, around 1-3 p.m.

Step seven: Identify the experiences contributing to your empowerment today or your future growth.

Day 7: Power Thought GENTLENESS

Step one: Say aloud,

Today, I will think about GENTLENESS

Today, I will feel GENTLENESS

Today, I will speak GENTLENESS

Today, I will act with GENTLENESS

Today, I will form patterns of GENTLENESS

Today, I will live in the reality of GENTLENESS

Step two: Think deeply about this thought for 60 seconds in a quiet, relaxed setting. Simultaneously, with your eyes closed, take a deep breath and exhale slowly. Do this seven times.

Step three: Embrace positive feelings and let them flow freely through you.

Step four: Write down the positive thoughts and feelings.

_____

_____

_____

_____

_____

Step five: Speak out the positive thoughts and feelings.

Step six: Take a 20-minute guilt-free, stress-free, and worry-free power nap, preferably in the afternoon, around 1-3 p.m.

Step seven: Identify the experiences contributing to your empowerment today or your future growth.

CHAPTER SEVEN

THE FIVE SMART WORK MATRIX LAWS FOR BUSY LEADERS

As an individual, you can incorporate all The Smart Work Matrix insights and wisdom into your daily life, but if you lead an organization, then these five laws are a must for you to follow:

1. Collaborate.
2. Network globally.
3. Build winning relationships.
4. Build up teams.
5. Do not manage.

#1 Collaborate

There's no greater feeling than being your own boss, but there is one big issue—the majority of leaders find themselves isolated and even alone. Leaders have defied the odds and pioneered for so long, but it is vital for such people to join other like-minded business leaders and Smart Work together. Partnering with other true Smart Work leaders is powerful and gives a person much more leverage and freedom.

#2 Network Globally

We have heard that the world is our oyster. It is one of the most powerful strategies to cultivate vast numbers of different networks. Get involved in strategic networks. It is not just what you know; it's also who you know and, more importantly, who they know. Great networkers have a pool of talent and robust networks that they draw on when a need arises.

#3 Build Winning Relationships

Being a winner is 80 percent likability. When people like you, they will trust you; when they trust you, they will listen to you. When they listen to you, they will follow you and support you. Be likable and spend your life building other people up. Invest time, money, and resources in people. As Zig Ziglar often said, "You can have everything in life you want if you will just help enough other people get what they want."

#4 Team Building

You cannot do it on your own. Great leaders know that not everybody on the team is the same. Therefore, they have three categories of people. I call these categories the Inner Circle, the Outer Circle, and the Outer Court.

a) The Inner Circle

These are three of your most loyal and faithful people, the handpicked ones that you like the most and they like you the most. They trust you and you trust them. They love and respect you and very seldom challenge you when you are wrong. They will stay with you through it all and will almost never leave you. These are the big picture people, the momentum builders, the action takers who are ready to run and conquer and plunder for you.

b) The Outer Circle

These are the ones who are the "detail" people. They execute the plan and make sure everything runs smoothly. Unlike your inner circle, these people are not that into you. They respect and admire you, but they are focused on the objectives, goals, and tasks, and on completing the mission. They will challenge you and point out your flaws and errors. They have a strong sense of responsibility to the entire team and clients. They are advocates for others, asking questions like "Are we a socially responsible team?" or "How can we be a better team for our clients?" They are invaluable because they are the counter-balance and will ensure compliance and help weed out all the wrongs that may be in your life and business.

c) The Outer Courts

These are the doers. They are not interested in office politics; they're just here to work and earn money. They enjoy working with you but always have an eye open for another opportunity elsewhere. They are not fully committed to you or loyal to the team. They are drifters and will always move on.

It's crucial to know which group people belong to. If you position a person in the wrong group, you will have more problems than you would like to have.

#5 Do Not Manage

Nobody likes to be managed. What people are looking for is someone who can lead. Most leaders will not admit it, but they are control freaks. Learning how to stop micromanaging is a challenge, and it's why so many leaders are stressed due to worry, anxiety, and fear. The result is that a leader is juggling several different projects at a time, and with so many irons in the fire, they are less effective. They live under the shackles of hard work instead of a life of Smart Work. I advise leaders to use this simple strategy to rid themselves of the craziness: Write down all your projects, even ones from years gone by, then follow this plan:

- Delegate – Some projects are urgent and time-sensitive. Select the right person ASAP and hand over control of the project to them. Don't undermine the person in charge or overwhelm them with constant requests and changes or demands. Trust them to deliver.

- Relegate – There are projects which may be important but not urgent. These must be correctly prioritized and set aside to lower priority.

- Eliminate – It's important to say goodbye to some projects or clients, no matter how close to your heart they may be. If it's eating up your time, money, resources, or peace, just get rid of it now and do not look back with any regrets. Just let go.

- Update – Set scheduled times to meet with your team to get updates and give insights. Nobody should be calling you out of these set times unless it's an emergency. It's also a good time to evaluate all your projects.

- Automate – We must use technology to simplify our lives. With today's rapid technological advancements, it is crucial that you not spend the time saved trying to learn about every new technology. Instead, find someone who can assist and do it for you.

EPILOGUE

As we conclude our journey through the realms of work, success, and fulfillment, it's important to reflect on the choices that shape our lives. The pursuit of true success doesn't have to be synonymous with relentless effort and exhaustion. Instead, we have the opportunity to embrace The Smart Work Matrix, a framework that invites us to redefine our relationship with work.

In this new perspective, we acknowledge that our worth is not measured by the hours we put in, but by the value we create and the joy we cultivate in our lives. Each of us has the power to break free from the constraints of overwork and carve a path that aligns with our passions and values.

As you move forward, carry the principles laid out in this book with you. Challenge the belief that busyness equals productivity. Seek harmony in your endeavors and pursue your goals with intention and grace. Remember, the choice between the burdens of hard work and the liberation found in smart work is yours alone.

May you embark on a journey filled with ease, fulfillment, and a deeper understanding of what it truly means to succeed.

Here's to embracing a life enriched by balance, purpose, and the freedom to thrive.

Your friend, Melvin Pillay

P.S. I'd love to hear all about your journey! Don't hesitate to drop me a line and share your thoughts with me at success@ melvinpillay.com. I can't wait to connect with you!

ABOUT MELVIN PILLAY

Melvin lives in Washington, DC., USA. He was born in poverty during the deep years of Apartheid in South Africa. Melvin had deep ambitions, which were only further fueled when his older brother, a law student and the economic hope of the entire family, tragically drowned.

Melvin moved to New Zealand and started in sales. For a long time, he was an abject failure. His boss secretly allowed him to sleep on the company floor as long as he was dressed and ready for work before any of the other employees showed up.

A major turning point occurred when Melvin discovered a Zig Ziglar cassette tape in the Auckland library. He rented it with his last two dollars (instead of eating that day) and dug into it with fervor. As he listened to Zig—and as he began to sense the spiritual foundation behind Zig's message—he made a vow: Someday, I will meet that man.

ONLY SEVEN YEARS LATER

Melvin found himself at a conference where the VP of Ziglar personally invited Melvin to be one of Ziglar's hand-selected trainers. Today, Melvin is one of only eight Platinum Zig Ziglar speakers/ trainers.

Melvin ties together three powerful streams: His Eastern culture and lineage, which uniquely honed his spiritual perceptions; the wealth and knowledge of having worked with leaders from around the globe; and the Zig Ziglar business culture, which empowers him to straddle many lines and move among many kinds of people.

Today, Melvin not only gives keynote speeches and trains and equips men and women to sell and run their companies with fervor; he also mentors them in the ways of intuitive wisdom and brings unique, fire- branded methods that must be experienced to be understood. His one- on-one personal Whiteboard Session is a must for those who carry large loads in today's high-pressure, high-speed economy.

www.melvinpillay.com

SMART WORK MATRIX WITH MELVIN

A re you ready to work smart with Melvin, unlearn the junk, un-grind from the rat race, understand yourself, and be free?

Melvin is available for keynote talks and has several Easy and Light consulting, coaching, and mastermind programs around the world.

The Whiteboard Session with Melvin Pillay

The Whiteboard Session is an immersive and transformative experience that integrates spiritual, mental, emotional, and practical dimensions. It is all aimed at optimizing personal development and preparing individuals for their destined path. This session is meticulously structured to facilitate the transition from potential to realization, offering profound insights into establishing a legacy that can endure for future generations.

A hallmark of the Whiteboard Session is its personalized approach.

Each session is distinctly tailored to the individual participant, ensuring that no two experiences are identical. The process is guided by divine revelation rather than solely depending on human wisdom or knowledge, fostering a spiritually enriching environment conducive to authentic growth and self-discovery. Over the past two decades, Melvin Pillay has engaged with diverse clients, including prominent business figures, innovative entrepreneurs, and influential government leaders. Through a unique coaching format, he has assisted individuals in unlocking their latent potential, guiding them toward realizing their fullest capabilities.

During the Whiteboard Session, participants can anticipate an in-depth engagement with the following key components:

1. *Exploration of Your Timeline:* Participants will collaboratively examine their life timeline, reflecting on past experiences, assessing their current circumstances, and envisioning their future aspirations. This exploration aims to uncover significant promises and purposes integral to the individual's life journey.

2. *Identification and Activation of Gifts:* Individuals will have the opportunity to identify their unique gifts and talents. More importantly, there will

be a focus on activating these strengths to foster enhanced confidence and clarity in their abilities.

3. *Assessment of Journey Conditions:* It is essential to understand the conditions that influence one's personal path. An evaluation of the physical, emotional, and spiritual environments in which individuals operate will be conducted to recognize factors that may facilitate or hinder progress.

4. *Uncovering Obstacles:* Participants will collaboratively identify barriers or obstacles currently impeding their progress. By illuminating these challenges, effective strategies can be developed to overcome them, ensuring a smoother path forward.

5. *Strategic Blueprint Development:* While examining visions and aspirations, a comprehensive strategic blueprint will be collaboratively created. This actionable plan will serve as a guide for participants to install lasting values and principles that will resonate for years to come.

6. *Foundation for Family Legacy:* In addition to personal fulfillment, emphasis will also be placed on establishing a robust foundational legacy for families and future generations. This component aims to empower participants to instill lasting values and principles that will resonate for years to come.

The Whiteboard Session transcends a standard coaching experience; it constitutes a significant step toward realizing one's God-given potential and establishing a legacy that positively influences others. Participants are encouraged to come prepared to explore, discover, and activate the possibilities within themselves.

LIFE AFTER SUCCESS

"**L**ife After Success" is a comprehensive program meticulously designed to optimize key dimensions for high achievers, public figures, CEOs, and business owners. This initiative aims to assist individuals in navigating the often-overlooked transition from achieving success to attaining true significance in their lives.

Uncover Your True Identity - Who am I?

Unlock Your Destiny – Where am I coming from?

Understand Your Authority – What am I anointed for?

Participants will engage with rich, thought-provoking content that explores the deeper meanings of success and addresses critical questions related to legacy and purpose. The program offers structured insights and actionable strategies for creating a lasting impact that transcends personal accolades and financial achievement. Through an integrated approach that includes workshops, reflective activities, and collaborative discussions, attendees will discover how to leverage their accomplishments to cultivate a greater sense of community, influence, and fulfillment.

By focusing on these essential areas, "Life After Success" equips participants with the tools and mindset necessary to craft a legacy that resonates and endures, ultimately leading to a more enriched and purposeful existence.

For more information please reach us at support@melvinpillay.com

www.melvinpillay.com

www.ingramcontent.com/pod-product-compliance
Lightning Source LLC
LaVergne TN
LVHW051239080426
835513LV00016B/1666